LABRADOR TALES

A Celebration of America's Favorite Dog

LABRADOR TALES

A Celebration of America's Favorite Dog

Written by:
John Arrington and Walter Zientek

Illustrated by:
Terry Albert

A Project of LABMED

Published by
Photo Restoration & Design

Published by
Photo Restoration & Design
46 Marlborough Road
North Haven, CT 06473
USA
email: ekearns@snet.net

For information about LABMED please visit
www.labmed.org

ISBN 0-9669159-3-3

Cover illustration © 2000 by Terry Albert
All illustrations in book © 2000 by Terry Albert

Printed in the United States of America

Second Edition

To all the ones who suffered and died
before we could help.

TABLE OF CONTENTS

LABS ARE...
By: Walt Zientek

Labs are Jeeps. And pick-up trucks and sport utilities. Labs are never Lincoln Towncars or Cadillac El Dorados. A Lab might be a Volvo Wagon, but never a Corvette.

Labs are John Wayne movies. Or Jimmy Stewart or even Meryl Streep and Clint Eastwood. I don't see a Lab as Jean-Claude Van Damme, Pamela Sue, or Steve Martin.

Labs are cabins in the woods overlooking crystal blue lakes. Labs are cottages on the beach with waves crashing in the front yard. Labs are a walk through a state forest, public park or nature trail. Labs are seldom weekends in the city, five star hotels or casinos.

Labs are soccer games, frisbees, hikes, jogs, and picnic lunches. Labs are not boxing, drag racing, French cuisine or formal wear.

Labs are a favorite pair of old, soft, worn blue jeans. A faded sweatshirt or a pair of sneakers. Labs aren't suits and ties, cocktail dresses and strings of pearls or Gucci loafers and custom made shirts.

Labs are steaks, cooked on the grill, chicken fried up by your Grandma, fresh caught bass and a cold beer on a warm summer night. They sure aren't paté or quiche or Merlot. Labs are clams on the half-shell, not Oysters Rockefeller.

Labs are lawnmowers and green grass, not subways and asphalt.

Labs are front porches, not fire escapes.

Labs are paperback books with dog-eared pages, not expensive first editions.

Labs are corny old songs that make you laugh and cry, not operas or symphonies.

Labs are never enemies or strangers. I guess I see them as friends. And family.

Labs are...

THE PERFECT LAB
By: Walt Zientek

The wise old Grandfather (aren't they all?) sat on the creek bank with his grandchild while the big dog romped in the water.

"Are Labs the best dogs?" the child asked.

"Sure are," he replied.

"What's the perfect Lab like, Gramps?" the child begged.

"Now that's a long story." (Aren't they all?)

"The perfect Lab is sleek and racy and full of energy and does a good day's work. Or it's solid and short-coupled and waits patiently in the ring.

The perfect Lab tracks a lost child, searches a collapsed building for survivors, returns ducks to hand or chases tennis balls across the back yard.

The perfect Lab is a hunter or an obedience trialer, a dog guide, a service dog or a couch potato.

The perfect Lab wears an e-collar, a blue ribbon or a little girl's Easter hat.

It swims in the ocean, the lake or a little blue wading pool. It rides in a mini-van, a pick-up or a motor home. It goes to matches, tests, shows, trials or Little League soccer games.

The perfect Lab catches butterflies or drug dealers. The perfect Lab helps a blind person catch a train. The perfect Lab is an old dog that's lived a full life, or a weak puppy fighting for every breath.

The perfect Lab lived 50 years ago.

The perfect Lab has yet to live.

The perfect Lab is being born today."

"Wow, Grandpa," the child said, "the perfect Lab sure is a lot of things!"

"Sure is," said the wise old man. "Sure is."

The Grandfather Series

THE PRIVATE LAB
by: Walt Zientek

". . . .Wow, Grandpa," the child said, "the perfect Lab sure is a lot of things."

"Sure is," said the wise old man, "Sure is."

The wise old grandfather whistled in the big dog and stroked its head.

"But the perfect Lab isn't the most important," the man said.

"It isn't, Gramps?" the child asked.

"Well," said the man, with a soft and far away look, "the most important Lab is the 'private Lab', and that, of course, is another long story.

The 'private Lab' can be a warm sweet memory. Perhaps a faded photo of a little girl with arms wrapped around a big black dog, or a long-ago little boy playing soldier with a chocolate or yellow best pal. The 'private Lab' can be the one in a litter that looks you in the eye and makes unspoken promises that only you can hear. The 'private Lab' might mean hunting trips with your Dad on cold October Saturdays, or a rescued dog found shaking, wet and frightened along a busy highway.

Sometimes, the 'private Lab' saved lives. Sometimes it slept with you when you were ill. The 'private Lab' is the reason for the best kennel names in the world. Sometimes the 'private Lab' is the one that raised your family and watched it grow up as it grew old.

An orphan, a mismatched pup, a Field Champion or a first time momma, lost in whelp, the 'private Lab' lives forever in your heart and mind. It becomes a part of who you are.

No matter how long you live, the 'private Lab' is your soul's companion dog. Just say, or even think its name... and you'll know that this is true."

The Grandfather looked away, took a deep breath and wiped some dampness from his sunburned cheek.

"Grandpa," asked the child, "where is your 'private Lab'?"

"Right here," said the wise old man, "right here."

Private Lab

MAN'S BEST FRIENDS
by: Walt Zientek

The wise old grandfather ambled slowly through the quiet October twilight with one hand on his grandchild's shoulder. The big black dog padded softly along side, lightly crunching autumn leaves.

"Gramps," the child asked, "dogs really are Man's Best Friends, aren't they?"

"Yes ... and no," the old man replied.

"Gramps, this is another long story, isn't it?"

"I'm afraid it is. Afraid it is.

You see, people live long, long lives compared to dogs. And people make lots of friends in lots of ways. If you're lucky, at least to me, you'll have many, many new Best Friends.

Sometimes, a Best Friend is a dog. Maybe a litter-runt the Momma doesn't want. You clean it and feed it and bond with it in a way like no other.

Sometimes, your Best Friend is your water dog, your dog guide or your ankle biter. Sometimes, your Best Friend lives with you in your home. Sometimes only in your heart.

But, sometimes, a Best Friend is two-legged. Maybe a squirrelly, dirty-faced kid in a Cub Scout's cap. Maybe a girl with freckles on her nose and bruises on her knees."

They climbed up onto the big front porch and sat down on an ancient glider swing.

"Yep, little one, folks are surely blessed. Best Friends can wear a big brother's gym shoes, a mother's apron, a nurse's cap, a policeman's badge or a construction worker's hard hat."

The old man absent-mindedly touched the big dog's head, turned a bit and fixed his eyes upon an old, worn, empty rocker that sat beside the swing.

"Sometimes your Best Friend wears a thick, leather collar around his neck. But, if you are truly blessed, your Best Friend wears a thin gold band around her finger."

The child thought for a moment and took the old man's callused hand.

"And sometimes, Gramps, if you are really, really, really blessed, your Best Friend wears a Grandpa's face."

For all the Best Friends of my life ... and yours.

THE LAST LAB
by: Walt Zientek

"Good-bye Grandpa! Good-bye Coal!" the child yelled as the car pulled away.

The wise old grandfather stood on the porch beside the big black dog, and waved until the car's tail lights disappeared from sight, then turned and walked through the front screen door. The dog's thick, short tail, slapped cheerfully against the doorframe as he entered with the man.

The two old friends made their way to a small, comfortable den, filled with the photographs that told the story of the old man's life. Photographs that told the story of his family that shrunk time to a moment.

"I guess you don't mind a long story, Big Guy?" the old man asked the dog.

The dog sat down and tilted his head as if listening to the man's every word. His tail swept the floor and his ears were cocked forward. He wore a silly Lab grin that said perhaps he had heard these stories before.

The old man picked up an old, yellowed photo and laughed quietly.

"This grubby little kid is me, with the first Coal." he said.

The big black dog tilted his head at the sound of the name.

"You sure remind me of him." the man went on. "He was always there as I grew up. He was my pal and my partner. A kid and a Lab understand each other. He used to walk with me to school every day. He swam the river with me and pulled me in against the current, many times.

He walked my paper route with me. He protected me for many years, and I guess I didn't know it then. He said good-bye to me at the train when I went into the army. I said good-bye to him too that day. Neither one of us knew that it was our last good-bye."

The grandfather scratched the dog beneath the chin. His eyes were far away.

"After the war it was an exciting time. Ma and me started raising a family. Couldn't let the kids grow up without a Lab. I did some work for a man in town whose bitch whelped a litter. One yellow guy in that pile. The man was going to drown him. No one wanted yellows then. I offered to take that dog instead of pay. Lord, was Ma mad at me! We needed a dollar more than we needed a dog.

That's the dog that raised the family. That dog was the best, most patient babysitter that I had ever seen. Thunder would let the kids do anything to him, but look out to anyone who threatened them. He would put himself between the kids and strangers. He'd look them in the eye and hold his stare. He never had to growl or posture. He knew his job and he did it well. He waited till the kids were grown before he died. It was like he saw that his job was done. I thank him every day."

The grandfather sat down heavily in the well-worn chair. The big dog put his head in the man's lap.

"It got so quiet around here when the kids were gone. Ma called me to the porch one day. She had this little brown pup in her arms. She said she couldn't stand to see me moping around all day, and so she got me one of those new chocolate Labs. Amber eyes and brown nosed, I laughed and laughed. Couldn't believe that was a Lab. Laughed so hard, we named him Happy.

Hap was that, if nothing else. I never saw a dog that loved life as much as him. He would run and jump and swim and play all day. He thought all company was there to see him. Maybe he was right. He didn't have to do anything around here but be a Lab. He sure was good at doing that.

He seemed to miss Ma as much as I did. He would find a shoe or dress she wore, and curl up and sleep with it. I would find him looking at her chair, like he was waiting. Wondering where she was. That chocolate guy is with her now, that much I am sure of."

The old man wiped his eyes and blew his nose and took the big black dog's face in both his hands.

"And then I found you," he said. "I had to have another Lab. I guess that I'm just a silly old man, but I needed another Coal. I needed one more big, black dog to walk with me. I needed a buddy like the one I had when I was a kid. I needed a friend to talk to when no one else is around."

The dog looked up at the old man, with wise, wise eyes.

"I needed another Coal," the man said. "I needed one last Lab."

The two friends sat there in that den for quite awhile. The grandfather didn't say another word. He didn't have to.

ECHO
by: Walt Zientek

"Hey Gramps? Gramps. Are you in there?"

The wise, old grandfather blinked open his eyes when he heard the voice. His hand reached down, automatically, to touch the dog that was no longer there. He felt a cold nose and a wet kiss against his fingers.

"What?" he mumbled as he looked down into a pair of sweet, dark eyes.

The little Lab tilted his head and wagged his short, fat tail.

For a moment, the Grandfather was confused. He saw, in his mind, another yellow pup, so very long ago. One named Thunder.

"Well Gramps," the strong, grown-up voice declared, "I guess Echo found you!"

The Grandfather looked up at his grandchild, now grown so tall and mature, and smiled.

"When did you get the pup?" the grandfather asked.

"Well," the grandchild answered, "that's a long story."

"Aren't they all?" the Grandfather replied. "Aren't they all?"

"You see Gramps, I spent an awful lot of time around here as I was growing up. Most of my favorite memories have to do with you and your Labs. I loved playing with old Coal. I loved looking at all these pictures. Most of all, I loved talking to you and learning from you. Learning about life and learning about Labs."

The old man smiled and realized that he still hadn't taken his hands off the pup. He scratched the little guy behind the ears.

"So," the grandchild continued, "When I was sure the time was right, I started doing some looking around. I knew I'd need a Lab to help me raise my own kids. I figured if Gramps had a yellow boy for that job, I should do it too."

"And you named him Echo?" the Grandfather asked. "Why?"

"I guess so many of your stories echo in my memory, that it just seemed to be the perfect name."

The very wise, very old Grandfather slid far forward in his big worn chair and held the pup's face with his two, rough hands. He looked at him and then looked up at his grandchild. His tired eyes scanned the faded photographs that filled the room. He found the pictures of Thunder, sitting with a group of kids. He waited until he could find his voice.

"I guess I taught you well, Kiddo," he said proudly.

The grandchild knelt down beside the Grandfather and the pup and put one hand gently on each.

"Thank you, Gramps," the grandchild said softly, "You sure did. You sure did."

TOGETHER AGAIN
by: Walt Zientek

"Good-by Gramps! C'mon Echo, let's go home."

The wise old Grandfather listened for the sound of the front door closing and settled down into his battered old chair. He smiled as he thought of his grandchild's new puppy.

"Labs sure are the way of life around here," he said to the empty house and quickly realized there was no one there to hear him, to answer back.

He suddenly felt very tired. Very old. Very alone. He put up his feet and closed his eyes and let the weariness overcome him.

***

The Grandfather felt warm sunlight on his face. He smelled the clean, fresh scent of early summer grass and slowly opened his eyes. He looked down at his hands and saw a younger man's skin, clear and tanned. He felt a sturdy tree against his back and solid ground beneath him. He looked up at an impossibly blue sky, accented with white, fair weather clouds. He saw ducks fly in perfect formation through that sky.

In the distance was a bridge that crossed a gentle river. People and dogs were playing in the fields around the bridge. There were dogs of every size and color and breed. All the folks were laughing and smiling and running with the dogs. Couples were holding hands and most had several dogs nearby.

The grandfather felt a sense of joy and calm. Far off to his left he saw two, big black Labs running toward him. He watched as the pair of familiar shapes grew near.

"Coal?" he asked aloud. "And Coal?" he said again.

He didn't understand. The dog of his childhood and the last Lab he'd ever owned were sitting side by side, tails wagging, just a few feet away. The dogs that he loved some fifty years apart were sitting together in this place.

"How can this be?" he questioned.

The two black dogs tilted their heads as if to listen and then turned and looked behind. A solid yellow dog was coming along the path. He stopped to greet all the children that he encountered on the way.

"Thunder?" the old man whispered to himself. "You always loved the kids the best."

The yellow Lab with soft, sad eyes, continued toward the man and took his place beside the two black dogs. He fixed his loving gaze upon the man and settled down.

The Grandfather knew that was his Thunder boy. He knew, even without seeing the little scar on his left ear. He knew, even though it was clearly impossible. The three big Labs, all turned their heads as one.

All four looked far off into the distance, at the figure of a woman walking with a chocolate Lab. The dog never left the woman's side. His eyes never left her face. His thick brown tail, never missed a beat, wagging so hard it looked as though his whole back would shake loose.

The woman raised her hand and smiled a smile the man knew so well and missed so much. She smiled the smile that stole his breath and his heart away, so very long ago. The sunlight caught the highlights in her hair and the smooth, fair skin of her face.

The woman and the dog called Hap stooped beside the others, a few feet from the man. No one spoke. No one moved closer. No one really had to.

The wise old Grandfather understood it all, just then. His heart filled up and spilled over as he smiled and nodded slowly. The beautiful woman smiled back and nodded in unspoken agreement. The four big dogs stood up and seemed to nod as well.

The man closed his eyes and felt the sun, once again, against his cheek.

***

"Gramps. Hey Gramps. Are you sleeping already?" the grandchild said softly. "I forgot my keys."

The wise old Grandfather got up from his chair and reached down again to touch the yellow pup.

"Have you got a few more minutes?" he asked. "I've got a story I want to tell."

The grandchild chuckled and asked, "Is it a long story, Gramps?"

"Aren't they all?" the Grandfather replied. "Aren't they all?"

... CARRY YOU
by: Walt Zientek

When I brought you home, I carried you.
I held you close and made a promise that day.
As I breathed in that sweet, soft, clean smell,
I promised to carry you, and keep you safe and well.
I laughed and spoke so quietly to you.
I taught you your name. You showed me your heart.
And I showed you mine, as I carried you, that day.

When I take you home, I'll carry you.
I'll hold you close, as I promised that day.
I'll breathe in that old familiar smell,
And keep my promise to keep you safe and well.
I'll cry as I speak so quietly to you.
I'll say your name. You'll show me your heart.
And I will lose mine, when I carry you, that day.

IN A MORE PERFECT WORLD
by: Walt Zientek
For animal rescue workers worldwide

In a more perfect world, there would be little need for Rescue, private or structured. Every person would have done careful research into breed and breeder, before making the decision to purchase a dog.

In a more perfect world, the law and the individual would see animals as more than property. Every dog would have a soft bed in a warm home, excellent food and inexpensive medical care.

In a more perfect world, there would be no puppy mills or animal shelters. Every breeding would have been meticulously planned and every puppy would have been spoken for, long before its birth.

In a more perfect world, every dog would have ten safe acres on which to run. Every owner would set apart some quality time each day to train and socialize and play with his or her dogs.

In a more perfect world, there would be no cruelty, fighting or abandonment. Every owner would look into the eyes of a dog and see a soul. Every dog would look into the eyes of a person and see a friend.

In a more perfect world, every dog would be a Heart Dog to someone.

AVOIDING THE WET SPOT
by: John Arrington

He didn't remember when it started. She didn't always do it. Make a wet spot, that is. But somewhere along the way, she began. It was little dribbles at first. On the kitchen floor surrounding her water bowl. Hardly noticeable and largely ignored. As the years passed, the dribbles turned into droplets and then to small puddles. In her final years the puddles grew to near natatorium size. So large were they that visitors were issued rubber boots and a personal flotation device at the door. Ok, I'm exaggerating! But the floor around her water bowl was always soaking wet.

Her drinking technique was interesting if not tidy. She adopted the usual stance and accomplished the lapping and swallowing the same as any other dog. There was nothing especially noteworthy about this. It was what she did next! She somehow filled the spaces between her upper teeth and lips with water. When she lifted her head and turned away from the bowl, the water drooled from her mouth on all sides. On a good day she could lay down a trail of droolly water from one side of the kitchen to the other, make a left turn and get half way to the middle of the living room before the well ran dry. Her owner did not approve. He was, nevertheless, without the power to stop it.

Where did she acquire such sloppy drinking manners, he wondered? Not from him. Not from the various cats who lived with them now and again. One thing about cats, they are very neat and tidy compared to Labrador Retrievers. Cats don't retrieve worth a damn and don't make you look macho when they ride in your truck, but they are tidy. Compared to Labrador Retrievers.

Making wet spots from kitchen to living room was bad enough! But after she mastered the fill up and drool deal, she discovered dancing. Human dancing. Dancing motivated by a shoe full of warm droolly stuff; the result of a direct droolly-water bomb hit by The Yellow Baroness. Cheddar strikes again.

The thrill of the dance was such that Cheddar was determined to teach every visitor how to dance. It became her standard greeting. Wag the tail, smile, and drool all over their shoes. For guests foolish enough to ignore her, she'd go back to the kitchen, reload, and launch a sneak attack on the drier foot. This never failed to attract their attention. She considered it the perfect way to get even with humans for all the times she'd been made to SIT or STAY or lay DOWN when she by golly didn't want to SIT or STAY or lay DOWN.

He always reprimanded her for drooling on the shoes of his guests. She expected it and even looked forward to it. It was a secret game they played. He always used his sternest tone of voice and banished her to the big cedar-filled bed on the floor near the woodstove. Part of the game was pretending it was a severe punishment. So she groaned when she lay down and always gave him an extra large dose of sad Lab eyes before the lullaby of human conversation put her to sleep. Cheddar snored and sighed when she slept. Another way of getting even with humans.

He liked to imagine she dreamed of greeting a door-to-door Evangelist wearing $900 wingtips while seeking alms for the poor. A thought that caused him to laugh a long silent laugh. And to grin from ear to ear. And to bend down and pet her from head to tail. He loved the Yellow Baroness and didn't mind at all avoiding the wet spot that surrounded her water bowl. And spread across the kitchen. And out into the living room. And sometimes on the shoes of his guests.

WRETCHED CATS
by: John Arrington

The old yellow dog began to quiver and shake and roll her eyes. She looked at the man who'd been her caretaker for nearly 15 years, and then at the cat lying down beside her. Lying down right there on HER bed. Right beside her. All her life she'd been taught not to chase cats and she always obeyed. Being this close to a cat made her nervous. There were rules about cats. Don't chase. Don't get too close. And now her man had brought this skinny wretched cat in off the street, fed it, and allowed it to go to the bathroom in a box. Indoors! It was uncivilized and outrageous behavior. Wretched cat. And now, after living with them for a month, this wretched thing was lying down on the edge of her bed, her brand new red bed with the heater in it. The new bed that made her aching joints feel so much better.

When she could stand it no longer, she struggled to her feet and moved away from her new heated bed. She stood for a moment and looked over her shoulder at the cat in her bed. She wanted to show the cat who was boss. Not supposed to chase cats, and barking indoors was forbidden too she reminded herself. It was a powerful temptation and resisting it made her tremble.

The cat moved to the center of the bed, curled up, and went back to sleep. The old yellow dog walked slowly across the room and sat down in front of her man. He was watching a football game on the television. She shook her head and the dog tags jingled. He paid no attention. She shook her head again with the same results. The Forty-

Niners were beating the Cowboys and he paid no attention to the old yellow dog until she sighed and rested her head in his lap. He stroked her gently and she sighed again.

It was then he noticed the cat on her bed. He arose from his chair, picked up the cat and sat back down in front of the TV. The old yellow dog stood for a moment and looked over her shoulder at her man. The Forty-Niners were beating the Cowboys and he didn't notice her sad Labrador eyes. The wretched cat was curled up in his lap and was making that peculiar purring sound. She wanted to chase the cat out of his lap where her head belonged. It was a powerful temptation but it was against the rules and the heated bed was finally empty.

Soon she was asleep on her new bed. She whimpered and ran as she slept. Her legs twitched and kicked. She chased the cat out the door and out of the yard. She stood by the fence and barked until the cat was gone from their house never to return. Life is good when you have a man and a warm place to sleep and can dream of saving the world from wretched cats.

SLEEPING TOGETHER
by: John Arrington

At bedtime, he turned off the lights and climbed the stairs. The yellow dog followed. At the top of the stairs she sat and watched him prepare for bed. When he was in bed and just before the lights went out, he always looked at her and said, "Cheddar, do you wanna get in the bed?" She always declined his offer. "Come on, Cheddar, up in the bed!" Again she declined and lay down and stared at him. They played a game of her invention. The rules of her game were strict. He knew this and accepted it. He grumped about it, but he had no choice. He found the game to be a nuisance, but comforting nevertheless.

The next move was his. He turned off the lights and feigned sleep. She rose silently and entered the room. Using all her guile and skill, she carefully climbed upon the bed. This was an important part of the game. She must not wake him, for if she did he would surely scold her and make her sleep on the floor. He just wanted to get it over with and get some sleep. He did not mind if she slept with him. He welcomed it and would never kick such a pretty girl out of his bed.

Nevertheless, they must play the game in strict accordance with the rules. She stayed at the foot of the bed for about 5 minutes. Then she moved toward him and stood over him and stared intently at the sleeping man. He could feel her stare, and as required by the rules, he remained motionless. She stared harder. He ignored her. She moved her head closer to his and breathed hot moist air from her nostrils into his ear. He pretended to awaken slowly. It was part of the game.

"OK! Under the covers!" He pulled back the comforter and lifted it to arm's length above him. She wagged her tail, turned, and burrowed her way to the foot of the bed. Only her nose was exposed to the night air. The proper rituals were observed. Her stealth and cunning had again won her the prized spot near his feet on the right side of the bed. All was right in her world and in his. In less than a minute they were sleeping together.

A LETTER TO CHEDDAR
by: John Arrington

Dear Cheddar,

I've wanted to write you a letter for quite awhile now, but I've been so busy. After we said good-bye, I got busy trying to find a puppy. It was the only way I knew to get over it. And since she came to live with me ... well, you know how much mischief a puppy can get into, don't you?

Remember the time we were at Terry's house? We'd been over at Fiesta Island and you'd run yourself ragged. When we got to Terry's you must have drunk two whole bowls full of water. After dinner we settled down in front of the TV ... and about an hour later you got up and went into her kitchen ... and started peeing ... and then walked down the hallway towards her bathroom ... still peeing ... then around the corner and into the living room ... still peeing ... and then back to the kitchen again ... still peeing. We were flabbergasted and cracking up too! Never saw so much puppy pee in one place in my life. Of course it was my fault. You obviously held it as long as possible. I should have let you out right after dinner. So Terry got mad at me. Remember?

But that's not the reason for this letter. I wanted to tell you I'm going to be all right. You know what a mess I was. You were lying there unable to get on your feet. And Dr. Willoughby told me it was time...that you'd given up and were ready. When I nodded my head yes, I saw the fear in your eyes. I was sure you thought I'd betrayed you. Now I understand that you weren't afraid for yourself, but rather for me. Now I know you thought I might not find another

Labrador to take care of me. Remember?

Cheddar, I couldn't stay and watch you die. I just couldn't. So I said good-bye while you were still my dog and then I got the hell out of there. I managed to hold back the tears while I was driving home, but when I walked into our empty house carrying your collar in my hand ... well, so much for all that macho crap! But now I'm getting used to the idea of remembering you instead of petting you. It's not the same, but it helps. So, no need to worry. I'm going to be all right

The puppy? I named her Chamois. She is a yellow Lab too. At first she seemed like such an outsider. Now she is becoming part of the place and a part of my life. I keep forgetting she doesn't know all the stuff about me you did. Like when I grab the car keys. She doesn't know to come to the back door, go pee, and get in the truck. You and I could get out of here in about 2 minutes. Chamois can turn our old routine into a 15-minute ordeal. But she's picking up on stuff like following me around the house and coming inside when I call her name. So don't worry, babe, I'm getting better everyday and we're gonna be all right.

Before I sign off, I just want to tell you how much I miss you and thank you for all those years and all those fun times we shared. Remember the backpacking trips in the High Sierra? Remember the first night you camped out and I had to teach you how to drink from a stream because you didn't know about water that wasn't in bowls? Remember how cold it was and how you snuggled down inside my sleeping bag and how you always wanted to sleep under the covers after that?

I'll never forget all of our adventures and I just want you

to know that even though I'm falling in love with Chamois, my love for you will not change. I know, I know, some days I get so busy with her, I don't think about you. But some days everything she does reminds me of you. So don't worry about us. We're going just fine now and we're gonna be all right.

Love you always,
John

WHOSE LAB THIS IS
by: Walt Zientek

Whose Lab this is, I think I know.
Her house is round the corner, though.
I do not think that she should be
On the streets, just running free.

Call her softly, if you can,
And show her you've an open hand.
We've got to get her quickly home,
It simply isn't safe to roam.

Do you know her? What's her name?
For it would be a perfect shame,
If she should try to run away,
Thinking this a game we play.

So we beckoned, soft and sweet,
And showed to her a tasty treat.
Because no Lab would be so rude,
To walk away from offered food.

Her collar held with a firm grip,
We started on our little trip,
Through a neighborhood we know,
Talking softly, walking slow.

To the neighbor's door we went,
A winter's afternoon well spent.
The dog was safely home that day,
So we hurried on our way.

We would've stopped and spent some time,
With our friends from down the line,
But we had schedules still to keep,
And miles to walk before our sleep.

BUTT WHAT??
by: Walt Zientek

"Honey, come quickly!" the wife called, "There's something wrong with the puppy!"

The husband dashed out into the yard and saw the little yellow guy racing crazily around and around. His eyes were glazed over, his ears were cocked slightly and his whole back end was practically scraping the lawn.

"I think it might be a seizure!" she cried. "He was just fine, sniffing around at everything, carrying sticks and playing with his toys. All of a sudden, like someone threw a switch, he took off!"

"I'll catch him!" yelled the man as he took off after the fifteen pounds of flying fur.

As he got within a few feet, the pup seemed to sense that the man was nearby and kicked on some invisible afterburners that easily doubled his speed and intensity and left the man sprawled face down on the lawn, grass stained and winded.

The puppy stopped running, picked up a small stuffed toy, gave it a very serious shake and continued, with clear eyes and quite normal posture, to sniff and explore the yard.

"Are you all right?" the wife asked. "Should I call the breeder? Should we take him to the Vet's?"

The man spit out a few blades of grass, got up slowly and tried to wipe the mess from his shirt and pants.

"I'm fine, I think." The husband answered. "I don't know what's wrong with him. Did he get stung by a bee or something? Is there something wrong with his back end?

Did something out here frighten him?"

"It's called 'Butt Tucking,' they heard a voice call out.

The side gate opened and a man walked through with a full-grown black Lab at his side. The pup ran over, rolled onto his back and then got up and licked the black dog on the face.

"Now they're pals," the man said. He unhooked the leash and let the big dog run.

"Go play with the puppy!" he called out. "But be EASY," he said, as though it was a command. The two dogs took off for the toys.

"Well neighbor, I guess this is the first time you've ever seen a Butt Tucking Lab."

"You mean there's a name for THAT? The pup is really O.K.?" the puppy's owner asked.

The second man laughed out loud.

"That, my friend, might just be the best definition of Lab behavior that you'll ever hear. Not every Lab will hunt or swim or retrieve on command, but for sure, every one will Butt Tuck."

"But what is it about?" asked the wife. "Is it because there is something wrong? Was he scared by something?"

"A Butt Tuck is the opposite of all that!" the neighbor answered. "It is a Labrador's physical reaction to the sheer joy of life. It is the instant release of energy in celebration of being a Lab. It is a thing of pure beauty to anyone that loves a Lab. It tells you that your dog can barely contain his joy. It tells you that he is feeling strong and young and full of life. I think there must be about a million other names for it. I guess every family calls it something else, until they hear about Butt Tucking. That name really says it all."

The black dog grabbed the stuffed toy from the pup and took off in a blinding sprint, with the puppy trying to keep up.

"There he goes," said the neighbor, "Showing the little guy how to do it."

"Wow, Butt Tucking," said the puppy's owner, "Something we should look forward to for a long time, I guess."

"For sure," said the other man. "But one day you'll notice that he hasn't done it for a while and you'll be a little sad. You'll give just about anything for him to be young enough to run for the pure pleasure of it. But watch him while he sleeps. You'll see his legs going like mad and his eyelids fluttering. Don't worry about him. You see, in their dreams they stay forever young and will Butt Tuck every day. After all, they are Labs."

LABRA-LESCENCE
by: Walt Zientek

"Jake, COME!"

"JAKE, COME!!"

"Dammit, Jake. Get over here!!"

"What in the world are you yelling about?" the wife called out to her husband. "I can hear you all the way downstairs."

"We are doing a little obedience training," the man replied.

"Very little, it seems, from the sound of things out here."

Just then, the rapidly-growing yellow Lab walked up to the man and did a perfect finish. He looked up with a self-satisfied expression and waited not so patiently for a treat.

The man reluctantly held out a small piece of well-nuked liver.

"Sure," he said, "Now you wander over! Mr. Look-at-Me-Doing-the-Job! Why don't you listen anymore?"

"Do you think that there might be something wrong with his hearing?" the wife asked. "I've noticed the he doesn't always respond to me inside. Sometimes when I call him nothing happens. I have to go looking for him. Then I find him in the shower eating the soap or the shampoo bottle. Sometimes I find him on our bed."

"Well, is he sound asleep when you go in?" asked the man.

"Errr, well, ...no, not asleep. He usually has a grip on your pillow with his front paws and he is, well, you know, like trying to have his way with the pillow."

The dog sniffed around the man's feet for a second or two and lifted his leg and let go a pretty good stream.

"What!!" the man bellowed. "What's the MATTER with you?"

The pup took off like a bolt of lightning.

"Not only is he deaf," the man complained as he tried to wipe his shoes off on the lawn, "but he is also losing his mind!"

"Should we call the Vet?" asked the woman. "Maybe he has a mental health problem. Do you think they have psychiatrists or something for dogs?"

"Labra-lescence. It's called, Labra-lescence." They heard a voice call out from near the gate.

"They all get it at this age," the neighbor said as he and the black Lab walked into the yard.

The yellow dog ran over and stopped just short of the pair. He sniffed from a distance and slowly approached the last few feet. The two dogs spent a few minutes looking each other over and soon ran off together to play.

"They will be O.K. now," the man said.

"So tell us about this, ... what do you call it?"

"Labralescence. You took Jake to puppy class, right?" the neighbor asked. "And he did great. Smartest darned dog there, I bet. Learned everything faster and did everything better than the others, is my guess."

"Well," said the woman with a little pride, "he was very good. We were thinking competition was probably right around the corner. But of course, he was still too young."

"Yep," said the neighbor. "And how about Basic Obedience? I figure he was the star of that show as well. Probably the youngest dog there, hanging on your every word, getting called on by the instructor to demonstrate each new trick. Am I close?"

"As a matter of fact," said the man, "he was easily the top dog. I started thinking how we could get into tracking work or hunt tests or maybe even some television jobs."

"Uh-huh, and now, if they ever have a need for a dog who can pee on your shoes, Jake is sure to get the job!" the man laughed out loud.

"Listen," he said, "don't you remember being fifteen or sixteen years old? How well did you listen to your folks? I bet you had other things on your mind that didn't involve doing what your parents told you to do. I'll bet that half the time you didn't even remember that you HAD parents, and the other half, you just pretended that you didn't."

"And I bet you pushed the boundaries more than a little then too. Got all full of yourself and didn't believe anything that you didn't experience first hand. A lot of good ideas back then, must seem awful foolish to you now."

"You mean the dog, Jake, is ..."

"Of course he is," the man replied. "Full of those hormones and chemical changes that rush through adolescent bodies and make mush out of adolescent brains. Testing himself and measuring himself against others. Getting that selective attention working. Feeling smug and insecure at the same time. Wanting to be the boss while knowing that he isn't."

"I bet he isn't doing very well in his class this time. Won't look at you, doesn't seem to hear the commands. Spits out the treats, just to show you how little he cares. Probably found a few females that seem very interesting."

"Wow, you're right!" the man said as he looked over at his wife. "That sounds exactly like Jake. Will he get better? What should we do?"

"Keep on working with him, and be consistent and steady and most of all, stay calm. Give him time to grow up a little. He'll be just fine. After all, he is a Lab."

URKAS?

by: Walt Zientek

"Honey!" the wife yelled. "Get over here right now! Something's wrong with Jakie!"

The husband dropped his lawn rake and bolted toward the dog.

"What's the matter?" he asked. "What's he doing?"

"He made a funny noise," the wife replied.

"He made a noise?" the man asked. "What do you mean, a funny noise?"

Just then they heard it. It was a little like the sound of a drum being banged, underwater.

"What the heck?" said the husband.

Then they heard it again. A sound like a toilet plunger working hard.

"His stomach is rolling up and down!" the wife noted with alarm. "Do you think he was poisoned? Did you leave your garden supplies around? Should we call the Vet?"

"He's just got a case of the 'Urka-Gurkas'." They heard a male voice call out.

"Just stand back and give him a second." The neighbor yelled as he came through the gate.

"A case of the what's?" the man asked. "Is he going to be all right?"

Just then the noise started up again. The yellow dog's stomach rolled and that distinctive sound resumed.

"Here it comes," said the neighbor.

The dog coughed, drooled a bit and gagged up a blade of grass. One blade.

"That's IT?" the woman asked. "All that noise and fuss for one blade of grass?"

"Sure. Or for a tiny piece of stick, a corner of a chew toy, two bites of cat food or just about anything else, can set off an episode of the Urka-Gurkas."

"But that name?" queried the husband.

"Listen to that sound, very carefully next time," said the neighbor. "The name sure does say it all. Urka-Gurka."

"Does this mean that Jake has a sensitive stomach?" the woman asked.

"Not at all. It is one of life's great mysteries. Labs tend to be very 'oral' dogs. Always carrying things around. Chewing on something. Swallowing all sorts of stuff. You never know what will set off the Urkas. Just keep paper towels on hand."

Just then Jake took off on a spectacular Butt Tuck.

"He sure seems O.K. now," the husband remarked. "Look at him go!"

The young yellow dog did several laps around the yard, grabbed a stick and tossed it into the air and picked it up again. He then ran over to his toys and chose a large ball from the pile. He rolled it out onto the lawn and pounced on it, sending it flying across the yard. He did this several times, while the people watched.

"I bet you never saw that game before?" the man asked his neighbor. "Jake invented that all by himself."

"Lab Soccer," the neighbor replied flatly. "Pretty common game they play. A little self-retrieving exercise. Most folks call it Lab Soccer. Gotta be pretty smart to put that game all together by themselves."

"But why does he keep the stick in his mouth?" the woman asked.

"Doesn't want to draw a penalty," the neighbor smiled

and answered. "I told you they were smart. After all, he is a Lab."

RETURN OF THE NEIGHBOR
by: Walt Zientek

"Honey," the wife called out, "come over here and take a look at Jake."

The husband rolled his eyes, pushed the snow shovel into the pile and walked over to his wife.

"What's wrong now?" he asked with little patience. "He looks just fine to me."

The tall yellow Lab buried his face in the snow, snorted loudly and looked at the pair with a silly grin on his frosted face.

"I think there's something wrong with his nose," the wife answered.

"Yeah, he's got snow all over it," the man grumbled.

"No," the wife said, "look at the color. It used to be so black. Now it is kind of red. Do you think we should call the Vet?"

"Oh that!" the man exclaimed. "That's called a 'Dudley Doright' nose," he answered smugly. "Something that happens to yellow Labs."

The wife gave her husband a look of disbelief.

"That doesn't sound right to me! Maybe we should ask..."

"You mean a Dudley Nose?" came a man's voice from the gate. "Jake does not have a Dudley Nose. He's getting a 'Winter Nose'; some folks call it 'Snow Nose'."

A big black Lab walked with the man into the yard. The two dogs wagged their tails, sniffed a bit and took off through the soft powder.

"I knew it was Dudley something," the husband mumbled sheepishly. "What's all this other stuff?"

"Well," said the neighbor, "some yellows have light pigmentation. It shows around the eyes and nose. It is like they have a chocolate Lab's pigment, with a yellow Lab's fur. Some folks really like that look, but it is a fault at shows. That's a Dudley Nose. Other yellows, like Jakie, have dark pigment, but their noses tend to turn dark red in winter."

"What can we do about it?" the woman asked. "What causes it?"

"Some say it's the cold; others say it has to do with sunlight. Some swear that you should never use a plastic food dish. Nothing at all to worry about," the man replied.

The yellow dog came over to the man, sat next to his foot and put all his weight against the neighbor's leg.

"Look at that!" the woman said. "See that? He isn't putting all his weight on his hip. I hope he's O.K.!"

"Labra-Leans," the man said with a chuckle. "Got more to do with personality than orthopedics. They love folks so much, they can't stand distance. I bet he'd climb up into my lap if I sat down."

The husband and wife exchanged a knowing look.

Just then, the two big dogs took off around the yard.

"Lab-Loops," the man stated.

"I thought that was Butt Tucking?" the man asked.

"Different body posture," the neighbor noted wisely.

The dogs calmed down and made their way over to the people once again. The woman wrinkled her nose and said, "Oh, Jake! Yuck! What in the world is that smell?"

"Labra-Gas," the neighbor said, while pinching his nose and laughing at the same time. "Not too much you can do about that, either!"

"Gee," said the husband, "Butt-tucks, Leaning, Looping, Gas and Urkas, and Labralescence! These dogs have their own language!"

"Of course they do," said the neighbor, "they are Labs, aren't they?"

THE CONVERSATION
by: Walt Zientek

(Telephone rings at 11:30 PM.)

Breeder: (Sleepily) Hello?

Everyman: Hi. I'm calling about Lab pups and someone said that you are the best professional breeder around here.

Breeder: Errr, well thanks, I guess, but I'm not a "professional" breeder. I'm a hobbyist breeder. I have a real job. I don't make a living by breeding dogs. It isn't my intent to...

Everyman: I see! Not good enough?

Breeder: No, that's not it at all. Breeding is an art, not a busin...

Everyman: I get it, slow market, huh? Supply and demand?

Breeder: (Patiently) No, not at all. I have a long waiting list and...

Everyman: Waiting list? How the heck long is this list? Christmas is coming and I want to surprise the wife with a blonde Lab! She's got three days off to train the puppy and all before we all go back to work at the Plant.

Breeder: (Still patient) Please be patient with me for a moment while I explain a few basics about buying and owning a dog, responsibility, training, reputable breeding policies, no Christmas placements and a little about Labs themselves. Sir? Sir?

Everyman: Huh? Sorry, I was getting something. (Loud 'snap' of a pop-top) Gulp. Ah!
Now, what were you saying?

Breeder: Well sir, Labs come in three colors: black, yellow and chocolate.

Everyman: So you don't have blonde? What about white or silver?

Breeder: You see sir, those are just descriptive names for various shades of the three colors. Yellow Labs can go from nearly white to fox red and chocolates come in a wide variety of shadings. What some are calling 'silver' has been declared to be a variety of chocolate and there is some controvers...

Everyman: So how much are you charging?

Breeder: Well sir, when someone has passed our buyer's screening criteria, it depends on whether they are looking for a show dog or a pet quality companion.

Everyman: Your what? Hey, I ain't looking to get it into Med school here or become the Pope or anything, I just want to get a dog as a Christmas present for Lulu-Mae!

Breeder: Well sir, all reputable breeders do everything to ensure puppy placement in excellent homes. We guarantee our dogs because we do all medical checks on the sire and dam. We co-own most show prospects and have a spay-neuter agreement on companion dogs. We also...

Everyman: A what-neuter agreement? Nobody takes the jewels off the boys around here! No way I'm turning my boy into a sissy dog!

Breeder: But sir, (exasperated) with the number of dogs abandoned to shelters and the number of unwanted litters produced every year, I feel...

Everyman: Hey, are your dogs registered with the AKC?

Breeder: All litters are registered with the AKC. You, if approved, would be allowed a 'limited' registration.

Everyman: Which means?

Breeder: Basically, that you could not breed your dog and register pups from that breeding because...

Everyman: Whoa Lady!! You mean to say that I fork over a couple hundred big ones to get a dog and you are going to tell me that I can't make a few bucks by breeding it?

Breeder: (Very exasperated) Yes sir. But the reasons for that are...

Everyman: Listen, lady, if I go down to the mall off of I-99 and drop in to the Puppy Playpen, will they have Labs? If I buy a Lab from them, do I get real papers? Can I breed that dog and make a buck?

Breeder: (Angrily) Yes! But then you would be supporting puppy mills and horrible, inhumane practices and...

Everyman: Lady, you don't have a dog ready for Christmas, you screen my application, you limit the registration, you make me snip the manhood right off of the dog. And to top it off, you are afraid of the competition. Why do you bother to advertise?

Breeder: Advertise? I don't advertise! I only sell through referrals and reputation! Sir, I have been VERY patient and have tried to educate you to the facts of reputable breeding and responsible ownership and it seems that we are getting nowhere! It is the middle of the night and I would like to try to get some sleep. I have a job to get to in the morning. Is there ANYTHING else I can do for you before I hang up?

Everyman: Well, there is just one more thing.

Breeder: What might that be, sir?

Everyman: What exit off I-99 is the mall?
(CLICK) (Dial tone)

Just a Pet

JUST A PET
by: Walt Zientek

I'll never feel the harness of a Service Dog. I'll never fly to earthquake sites. I'll never do airport duty. I'm just a pet.

I'm not as pretty as a show dog or as driven as a trialer. I go to school, but not to competition. I'll never pass on my genes. After all, I'm just a pet.

You won't find my pictures in the famous books or read my story in the popular journals. The color of my nose, the shape of my tail or the thickness of my coat is not that important. Remember, I'm just a pet.

Just a pet. A member of the family, a part of the pack. My photos are in the album. I'm wearing reindeer antlers and silly sunglasses! I get special birthday cakes and dog-friend parties. They take me to the beach, park, lake and forest.

My people worry over me. They get my shots and check-ups done. They spend more time on my diet than they do on their own. I don't know why they do it. I'm just a pet.

Just a pet, but they treat me like a person. They talk to me, brush me, train me, brag about me, hug me and sometimes even cry over me.

And I can't give them anything back. I mean, I'll baby-sit and guard the house and put up with anything my kids dish out. And just maybe, sometimes I let them see something of themselves in me, in my gentleness, my courage, and my pride. Oh sure, I love them without regard to anything. Maybe because our time together is so short...I don't know, I'm just a pet.

GIVING UP LABS
by: Walt Zientek

Some days are like that. They just seem to drain the life out of you. This was one of those days.

The man pushed back into his chair and grunted, trying to relax and unwind.

"Look at Hershey," he heard his wife say.

The man forced open one weary eye. The big chocolate Lab was doing his famous "staring" thing.

"He needs his run," the wife said.

The dog tilted his head, clearly listening, thinking, anticipating.

"I've got to give up Labs," the man thought to himself.

"He waits all day for you to get home, just to run and chase a ball," the wife added.

"Yeah, yeah," the man thought. "I'm definitely getting out of Labs." The man forced his swollen feet back into his shoes, pulled on his coat, crunched a rumpled cap onto his head and moved toward the back door.

"Come on Useless!" he growled.

The big brown dog leapt straight up and hit the ground running, his heavy tail painfully swatting the man's leg as he ran by.

"Ow!" the man barked. "I'm really giving up Labs!" he thought.

The chocolate dog ran through the sloppy snow with wild abandon. Tail down, rear end nearly hitting the ground, he circled the yard several times, kicking up mud and snow and grass.

"SLOW DOWN!" the man yelped. "My lawn has had it!" he snorted.

The dog dug out a grubby ball from beneath a naked shrub and brought it to the man. He gently nudged the man's hand until he took the ball and threw it. The game went on until the dog grew tired and the man's shoulder grew sore.

* * *

The woman had started to worry. They'd been gone a while now. She peeked out the back door and saw the two sitting on a lower step. The man's left arm wrapped around the dog's back, speaking softly as his right hand gently cleared snow and mud from the big dog's gray speckled face.

"What are you and Hershey ever talking about?" the woman asked.

The man and the dog turned to her voice.

"We're just talking about giving up Labs," the man said in his most serious voice.

And then he smiled.

The dog just smiled.

A DIFFERENT CONVERSATION
by: Walt Zientek

(Telephone rings at 7:00 PM)

Breeder: Yes?

Buyer: Hello, my name is (blank) and I was referred to you for information about buying a dog.

Breeder: And?

Buyer: Well, I guess I am interested in purchasing a chocolate puppy.

Breeder: How much show experience do you have?

Buyer: None, actually, I am looking for a great companion dog and...

Breeder: (impatiently) Hold on. (pause)

Assistant: (impatiently) Yes?

Buyer: Hi, I was calling for information about a chocolate Lab puppy and you were highly recommended.

Assistant: OF COURSE we were! We at Avarice Kennels have produced hundreds of conformation champions. (suspiciously) How did you get our number. We are NOT in the book.

Buyer: You were recommended by Mr. (blank). He owns one of your pups and gave you glowing praise.

Assistant: I'm quite sure he did. How much show experience do you have?

Buyer: As I told the other person, we are just a family, with a fenced yard, two great kids and lots of love...

Assistant: So, you do NOT intend to show? We are a show kennel. All of our dogs are bred to the strictest conformation standards. We do not invest thousands of dollars on clearances and stud fees and show costs to have our work end up in someone's backyard. We expect our buyers to campaign our puppies around the country to keep our name visible in the specialty circles.

Buyer: But certainly every dog you produce can't be show quality. You must have some that will be great pets. I have done some research, purchased a crate and have several good puppy books here already and...

Assistant: I'm sure you have. But as I said, we are a show kennel and that is our interest. If you were to consider competition, we might consider co-ownership with us retaining breeding rights and kennel name. Our desire is to protect our interest.

Buyer: I thought your desire was to produce great dogs and to better the breed?

Assistant: SIGH! Yes, yes, yes, that too (very impatiently). I am quite sure that we do NOT have anything that would suit your, errr, needs. Is there something else? We are very busy.

Buyer: Could you tell me the exit off I-99 for the Mall?

WONDER DOGS? ....I WONDER
by: Walt Zientek

I wonder....

.... how an 80 lb. dog gets on the refrigerator?

.... how a 'super premium' food can ruin a dog's digestion, but a chipmunk, an entire turkey, 7 cupcakes with wrappers, rhubarb pie and a Bic lighter, doesn't?

.... why 'labragas' is funny, but 'husband gas' is gross?

.... why the smallest women own the largest dogs?

.... where old tennis balls go?

.... how male dogs always know which shrubs are the most expensive?

.... why Kaopectate is considered a 'staple' to some show folks?

.... why people always give their dogs way better names than they give their kids?

.... how a dog 'always' finds the dog-hater in the crowd?

.... why the 'breed standard for temperament' is usually a good descriptor of the owner?

.... why the smellier the substance, the longer they roll in it?

.... why, once you really get into dogs, cleanliness is not quite as close to Godliness as it once was?

.... why slurpy dog kisses are always good, no matter what they were licking 5 minutes ago?

.... why dogs have the best web sites?

.... why dogs chose to bond with humans?

.... why the Lord was kind enough to create the dog?

AND....

.... why He was cruel enough to give them all such a very short time?

Black Dog Studio

CHAMOIS – MY NEW BEST BUDDY
by: John Arrington

Cheddar, a yellow Lab, was my best buddy for nearly 16 years. She loved to ride in the truck. Jingle the keys and she'd do spinners and run to the back door and whimper and wag and tap dance with her front feet until I let her out. As soon as the door to the truck opened, she'd leap in and take her place in the passenger seat, eager to go wherever I might take her. She went everywhere with me.

One day, sometime after her twelfth birthday, she tried to jump in the truck and couldn't make it. She could get her front legs up on the seat, but the years and the arthritis had taken their toll. From that day forward, whenever we went in the truck, the routine never varied. When I opened the door, she'd jump those front paws up on the seat, look at me over her right shoulder wagging her tail with excitement, and then give the biggest jump she could manage to help me out when I lifted her in.

This weekend I took Chamois for a ride in the truck. Up until now I had to catch her, pick her up and put her on the seat or in the crate. Sunday, after I got Little Ms. Wiggles into her harness, we went out to the garage and when I opened the door to the truck, she jumped her front paws up onto the seat ... she was barely able to reach it, but managed it nevertheless. Without thinking, I bent down as I had so many hundreds of times for Cheddar and lifted her little behind up and onto the seat. As I was lifting, I was suddenly aware of how light and small she felt and immediately remembered lifting the back half of Cheddar's 70 lbs. As I was buckling Chamois into the seat belt, tears welled up in my eyes and a giant lump formed in my throat. I was remembering the last time I'd lifted Cheddar into the truck. It was for a ride to the Vet's ... a ride she was unable to come home from. Cheddar ... oh what a dog! Oh what a love affair. Bigger tears and wetter cheeks.

And then a tiny, quick pink tongue licked the tears from my cheeks and everything was all right once again. You see, I have a new best buddy now!

DAWN PATROL
by John Arrington

4:49 AM ... Chamois raises hell in her crate. I drag my sleepy buns out of bed. On with the slippers, on with a sweater, on with a pair of sweat pants. Ok, Chamois, you wanna go out? I open the door to the crate and turn and shuffle toward the dark hallway. Before I can find the light switch, a yellow energy rocket explodes down the hallway towards the kitchen. An instant later my feet are the course markers in a high speed slalom event involving Chamois coming back down the hall at a high rate of speed preceded by Doolittle the cat. Doolittle stops and hides behind my legs for protection. Chamois' brakes are inadequate for Doolittle's unexpected stop and she crashes into my ankles nearly taking me down. A furious bout of Doolittle hissing and batting with the front paws at Chamois ensues. Doolittle was declawed when I rescued her and is an inside cat. Bat, bat, bat, hissssss. All to no avail 'cuz there are no claws to slash open Chamois' nose ... so Chamois thinks it's a love tap and whaps the cat right back with her paw. The cat does not interpret this as a love tap nor does she like it and makes a high-speed strategic withdrawal to the bedroom where she knows she'll be safe on top of the bed. Chamois gives chase, nearly knocking me over again. The time is now 4:50. I've been out of bed for almost a minute and have nearly been knocked on my butt twice. Did I tell you I'm grouchy when I wake up?

"Come on Chamois ... you wanna go out," I say to the darkness in the hallway. I hear the thundering hoof beats of a stampeding Lab puppy and try to guess if she'll pass on my left or right side so I can get out of the way. I guess wrong. Ouch! Chamois has a Nike in her mouth and whaps the back of my leg with it as she passes at warp factor 6. A few seconds before 4:51 A.M. we're at the kitchen door and I've managed to find the light switch. Chamois is sitting in front of the door, the Nike is forgotten, and as I open the door she looks up at me, gives me a killer dose of Lab eyes, and wags her tail with puppy enthusiasm as if to say, "Where have you been, old man, I gotta pee," and sprints out to her favorite spot. Did I tell you I'm grouchy when I wake up?

By 4:54, she's peed and pooped and raced back inside for food. At 4:55 I put a bowl of food on the floor and make a halfhearted effort at making her wait for a release before she dives into the food. By 4:56 the food is gone, gone, gone. By 4:56:01, she's racing down the hall to see what the cat is up to. I catch up and while Chamois is standing up on hind legs and peering over the edge of the bed at Doolittle, I capture her and steer her back to the crate in the corner and say, "Box" and like the little angel she is, she walks right in and starts gnawing on a Nylabone. By 4:58 I'm back in bed and all is quiet on the Western Front.

THE HUMBOLDT PET FUR DEPOSITORY AND BANANA SLUG RANCH

by John Arrington

In the best of times, I'm not fully awake until about 10 A.M. and that's when I crawl out of the sack around 8 and have the benefit of a hot shower, a can of Diet Coke and a handful of aspirin. And now this puppy has me out of bed at 5 A.M., ferchrissakes, for her early morning comfort break.

So there I was stumbling around in the cold drizzly pre-dawn darkness waiting for my little angel to do her business. I had a big wad of paper towels and was ready to pounce on the pile before it got a chance to start steamin'. Light from the kitchen window cast dim shadows across the grass and I could barely see Chamois pointing. Pointing? Yeah, you know, head up, back tilted at a 45-degree angle, tail straight and quivering ever so slightly (some call this squatting ... No ... it's a Lab's way of pointing). Two bobs of the tail signaled she was finished. I yawned and dropped the paper towels over the long cylinder laying in the grass at my feet, bent down wrapped my hand delicately around it so as not to moosh it into the grass, and lifted it gently off the lawn.

"Unnnnuuuuhggg," I yelped. It was moving! Yes! Moving! My primal moan scared the heck out of Chamois and she was running toward the back door and safety. I threw the moving poop to the ground and leaped back-ward. A major adrenaline rush coursed through my body. I was instantly and totally awake and had a 3-digit heart rate. My hands were shaking and my brain was conjuring up all kinds of Sci-Fi body snatcher images. Aliens were breeding in my poor little puppy's abdomen. Alert the cops and the Air Force. Batten down the hatches. Call the vet. CALL THE TABLOIDS! I looked down at where the paper-towel-wrapped alien lay and started to breathe again.

"Whew! Relax, John, it's OK. Everything is going to be all right," I said to myself. Instead of aliens or something equally sinister, I'd picked up a giant Banana Slug! It was about 6 inches long and covered in slug slime. And lying right beside it was what I'd been after in the first place.

CHAMOIS AND THE BACHELOR
by John Arrington

Now you've gotta understand, I'm a bachelor. Always have been. And a bachelor does a lot of things differently than a man with a woman to take care of him. Toilet paper is a good example. Every place I go where there's a woman in command the toilet paper is stored on those little roller thingys ... you know the little deal on the wall that looks like a convenience handle for the handicapped. Not at my place. Toilet paper here resides on the floor next to my right foot when I'm using the facility and on the counter when I'm not. I like to pick up the roll and take two or three turns around my hand ... makes a nice, easy-to-use efficient bundle. But all that may soon have to change ... you see I have a female in my life with toilet paper on the mind. The female in question is Chamois, my 12fi-week-old Lab pup.

This morning after her 5 A.M. rest stop in the back yard, I shuffled back to the bedroom, put her back in the crate and answered an urgent call to cast my ballot in favor of requiring poodles to turn in their blow dryers and get sensible haircuts. As I sat there with my sweat pants around my ankles and nearly asleep, a tiny blond head appeared followed by the rest of Chamois. My first thought was ... John if you want the puppy to stay in the crate you should latch the door. My second thought and my first attempt at speech that morning were one and the same. Chamois was stalking the roll of toilet paper at my feet.

"NOOOOO," I mumble-shouted, but it was too late. She pounced on the roll, gripped it in her mouth and took off in a butt tuckin' sprint. This presented me with only one option because Chamois had the last roll of paper in the house and if you will forgive my indelicacy ... I was in dire need of it.

I stood up, and in my first try in almost 56 years at walking like a baby with a load in its pants, I almost killed myself. In my haste to get the paper before Chamois rendered it unusable, I'd forgotten about the sweat pants ... you remember the sweat pants around my ankles, don't you? Of course I tripped ... but the fat little Gods of Disaster must have been sleeping because somehow I managed to avert a fall.

Down the hallway and out to the living room and kitchen I waddled. Chamois was nowhere in sight. Back down the hallway. Nope, not in the office, not in the guest bedroom, not in the guest bathroom. Where was she? Ahhh, under my bed. Munching on the toilet paper. Chewing up little wads of it and spitting them out so she could tear off another hunk. I won't take up your time with the saga of retrieving the roll from under the bed, nor how I got it back from Chamois, but I ask you this: have you ever tried to use Lab-spit-soggy toilet paper that's as full of holes as a lace doily?

Maybe I'll have to start using that little roller thingy on the wall. Or find a woman who wants to take on a big project.

CHAMOIS AND THE WADING POOL
by John Arrington

It was time for Chamois to get her feet wet and I damned near blew my brains out trying to inflate the little plastic wading pool. When it was inflated and filled with water to a depth of 2 inches, I walked her up to it. She sniffed at the vinyl, tasted it, and wandered off to another corner of the yard to sniff some other, presumably more interesting, stuff. I called her. She ignored me. I got a tennis ball and bounced it a couple of times. She came running. I tossed the ball in the direction of the pool. She retrieved it. I tossed it in the pool. She ran toward it, slammed on the brakes and looked puzzled. One foot tentatively pawed at the water. She barked at the ball. More pawing. More barking. She tasted the water and pawed and started to get excited. A moment later both front feet were in the water. It startled her and she jumped backward and out of the pool. A hot lap of the backyard at butt tuck speed ended in a screeching halt at the edge of the pool. I fished out the ball and tossed it away from the pool. Another retrieve, right back to me and a full circle around me and another hot lap of the yard with the ball in her mouth. I called, clapped my hands, and she hauled buns from the furthest corner of the yard, circled behind my feet and offered the ball to my waiting hand.

"GIVE," I said. She released the ball and I tossed it in the pool. This time she gingerly entered the pool with all four feet, snatched the ball, and trotted back to me, head held high, tail wagging and with that, "Boy, did I do good," look of pride written all over her face. We did it two or three more times and each repetition brought a little more confidence in her entry into the water. It was time to get my camera.

When I returned to the scene, Chamois was pawing at the water, jumping in and out of the pool, and having a great soaking wet time. I wanted a picture of her reaching forward with her mouth to retrieve the ball. I sat on the ground, carefully framed the picture, tossed the ball in the pool and she was off like a rocket. And she returned like a rocket too and leaped into my lap. The force of her landing in my lap and against my chest rolled me over on my back and in an instant my 22-pound yellow bowling sponge had soaked me from chest to crotch with cold water. She dropped the ball and attacked my face with muddy gritty slurpies. And I laughed and laughed and laughed.

CHAMOIS DISCOVERS ICE CREAM
by John Arrington

She stood next to my chair on her back legs with front paws draped over the armrest. By standing on her tiptoes, she could push her muzzle against my arm to get my attention. I tried to ignore her, but she was insistent.

"Pay attention to me ... nudge ... nudge .... nudge," she was saying.

I looked away from the TV and into her dark eyes. Those dark brown eyes. Those pleading Lab eyes. You know the look! So insistent. So pitiful. You know, that sad-eyed Lab look that says, "Why are you being so mean?" Or "Why don't you share your treat with me?" Or "Why are you leaving me behind?" Or "Why are you petting that old cat, anyway?"

I looked away and gouged another spoonful of ice cream out of the cardboard container. Her eyes followed the spoon from carton to mouth and back to carton. Nudge ... nudge ... nudge. I ignore her and take another bite. Again her eyes follow the spoon. She's never eaten ice cream. Is she interested merely because I'm eating something or does her little black button nose detect a delicious aroma ... an aroma too subtle for my human nostrils to detect?

I continued to work on the pint of ice cream, now nearly gone. She's becoming more insistent. Nudge ... nudge ... nudge. When I make eye contact she jumps up and down on her back legs and wags her tail furiously. What do you want Chamois? Nudge ... nudge, and her eyes dart back and forth from mine to the ice cream. Her ears are on full alert and her expression has changed from pleading to anticipation. A little squeak and a tiny high-pitched bark escape from deep inside her chest.

I push her away from the chair. "Chamois, SIT!" Her little butt moves smartly to the carpet. "Do you want to lick the carton?" More furious wagging and she leaps from her sit and lands feet first in my crotch. A reflex arch and a wince save me from the soprano section ... but just barely. "Chamois, SIT!" She reacts to the command by running back to the side of the chair and announces her return to the paws-on-the-armrest position with an eardrum shattering yelp-bark. Maybe I shouldn't tease her.

"Chamois, SIT!" Another loud yelp ... the Lab puppy equivalent of flippin' me off. But I am as determined as she. After a couple more tries I win and Chamois gets the carton to lick. Her head almost completely disappears into the bottom of the carton and she licks and wags at high speed. And no wonder ... it's her first ever taste of Cherry Garcia!

Chamois Discovers Ice Cream

SYNERGY
by Walt Zientek

There was no alarm clock. No ringing. Wasn't any need. Wasn't any reason. The old woman blinked herself awake. And remained still. Takes some time to get going these days. Have to take inventory. Make sure all the parts are working. The dog is awake. Have to get up.

The old dog blinked herself awake. Her mistress was awake. She knew it. Didn't hear or see her. No need to.
After all these years, she just knew it.
Glad her mistress took her time.
Her old parts were working fine, but took a little while to loosen. Have to get up.

The woman shuffled down the hall.
About midway, she stopped to open the back porch door. Let the old girl out. Can't make her hold on forever. The woman made her way to a tiny bathroom. Moving along a little faster now.

The old girl wobbled down the six worn steps.
About midway, she stopped and sniffed the familiar ground. Feels good to move around. She made her way to her favorite spot. Feeling a little looser now.

The woman put the water on to boil.
Got to feed the old girl. She loves her breakfast.
Lord, she still looks forward to her food.

The dog sniffed out the carelessly thrown newspaper. Here it is. Must be careful with it now.
She so looks forward to it coming in!

So much to do today. Errands to run. The old girl hates being left alone.

The woman bent down. Low.

So she could put her face beside the dog's.

Touch the soft gray muzzle with her cheek.

   Stay with me today? Leaving? She hates to leave me.

The dog stretched her body upward. High.

So she could put her face beside the woman's.

Touch the soft silver hair with her cheek.

   The woman settled into bed. Quiet. Dark.

She lay very still, listening. Sound of steady breathing.

Dog is asleep.

Silly how we get attached.

Good night old girl.

   The dog settled into bed. Contented sigh.

She lay very still. Listening. Steady breathing.

The woman is asleep.

Silly how much we care.

Good night old girl.

FULL CIRCLE
by Walt Zientek

She had come to hate autumn. Cold and gray. The colorful leaves, now a daunting, nuisance chore. The old clichés were true. The shortened days. The dying of the year. A time for endings.

She dropped a tape into the VCR. Old home movies made into video. A lifetime passing even faster than it really does.

The screen showed her own backyard. In autumn. In the corner stood the swings. She smiled.

"God," she thought, "how long ago was that?"

A giant pile of leaves had been built nearby. A leggy pup ran into view. He stopped, sniffing the air and dove head first into the pile. The leaves came alive with motion.

The pup emerged. And then a little girl with long blond hair. And then a smaller even blonder girl wiggled from the pile. The three young ones laughed and jumped and ran around the leaves. One by one, they looked up and faced the house.

"Hi Mommy!" they shouted on the silent film. They waved and the pup ran off the screen.

* * *

"Hey Mom! Hey Mom! Come and look at the dog!" she heard from out back.

She stepped out onto the porch and looked out toward the shed that had replaced the swings.

A giant pile of leaves had been built nearby. A different, leggy pup ran into view and dove into the pile. A tall, young woman with long blonde hair clapped her hands. A second slightly younger girl, ran over to join the fun. The three young ones laughed and jumped and danced around the leaves. One by one, they looked up toward the house.

"Hi Mom!" the girls shouted as they waved.

She raised her hand and waved back and smiled her biggest Mother's smile. But she didn't answer back. She didn't quite trust her voice.

Full Circle

A SHORT WALK
by Walt Zientek

They would have held hands. The man with the great, warm smile and the woman with the secret grin and far away look in her eyes. They would have held hands, but their hands were busy holding the leads of the two big dogs as they strolled the quiet streets of the sleepy village.

The two dark-coated dogs turned their noses to the breeze that drifted from Lake Erie. The man turned his smile to the faces of the many friends that greeted them that day. The woman turned her mind to the memories that those faces brought to mind.

The dogs could smell the water on the air and they remembered days of swimming and running and the joy of being dogs. The man remembered all the times he spent with friends. The laughter and sometimes the tears that brought their lives to-gether. The woman, remembered the faces of the friends, the way they were so long ago.

When they stopped to talk, the dogs would sniff and wag their tails. The man would shake hands or tell a joke. The woman would find the sparkle in their eyes, look for the honesty in the faces.

So they walked that day around the little town.

And as the shadows grew longer and the day grew cooler they walked a little closer. They would have held hands. But they didn't have to.

BALNORIA NIGHT
by Walt Zientek
for Deirdre

Boy, it was quiet. "Too quiet," she thought as she headed out into the darkness.

The strong spotlight faded quickly as she made her way out back, leaving her alone in the blackness. She flicked on the powerful flashlight and scanned the grounds for the hens.

Inside the house, the dogs paced nervously from window to door, the hair prickled up on their backs, their ears set forward to catch any sounds. The big yellow boy tensed every muscle in his powerful body. And listened. And sniffed at the air.

Fear of coyotes made her keep the dogs in at night, though she'd feel safer if they were close by. She worried more about their well being than her own, so she locked them safely in.

"No coyotes tonight," she thought to herself. "Too quiet."

As she moved farther from the house and deeper into the darkness, the dogs grew even more agitated and quickened their pacing. A low growl escaped the big boy's throat.

"Here chick-chick," she cooed softly, aware of the beads of sweat forming between her shoulder blades and beginning to run down her back.

She shuddered. With all the heat she felt very cold. She shook again, as much from nerves as temperature.

Now, all the dogs were growling steadily and staring out the windows

She felt watched and she froze.

"Dear Lord," she said aloud. "Dear Lord."

The fat hens appeared in the beam of the flashlight and made their way right to her. She grabbed them up and swung the light around. All seemed well. A coyote howled far in the distance. The buzz of insects filled the air and she turned for home.

Inside the house the dogs settled down, except the big one. He waited patiently for her return.

"Hi Herc," she said, as she crossed the threshold to the sight of the happily wagging tale.

"Glad to see me?" she asked.

The big dog just stared out into the darkness as she shut and locked the door.

CHOCOLATE CHIP COOKIES FOR SANTA
by Walt Zientek

The little pup was confused and frightened. She was such a precious girl. A delicate thing with soft golden eyes. She tried so hard to do the things her people wanted. She almost always went outside on time. She went to school and practiced real, real hard, even when she wasn't sure of all the words. She was a Lab after all, and her people were most important to her.

Maybe she played too hard? Maybe she should have tried to be a bigger girl and not get so excited by her toys and balls? Maybe she kissed too much? Maybe people really don't want doggie kisses all the time? Maybe happy tails knock over too many things? Maybe she should have tried harder?

She wondered if it was the clothing. Perhaps she should have learned to leave the socks alone? The underwear! The pantyhose! That silly skinny string that tastes like mints! She knew now why things had turned out this way. She had been so bad, even though she had tried to be good.

Christmas time was coming and at first all had seemed so wonderful. Lights and garland and tinsel and a big, green tree, right inside the house! Presents being wrapped and hidden and excitement in the children's eyes.

And then the talk of a big, jolly man that rides a magic sleigh and comes to visit all the boys and girls. Santa Claus, sliding down the chimney, leaving gifts behind. It seemed a wonderful time of year.

Then she heard the words that told her she was bad. "We have to leave Chocolate Chip cookies for Santa this year," the momma person said. "To take away with him on his sleigh."

The little golden-eyed girl was sad. But because she was a Lab, she accepted her fate. That quiet Christmas Eve, she took her place by the hearth and waited for the time to come. She only blamed herself.

"Cookie. Wake up baby girl." She heard the momma whisper. "Merry Christmas Cookie!" the little girl squealed. "Look, Santa has come and eaten the snack we left him! And he even left some presents for you! Look! They say, 'To Chocolate Chip Cookie, the best little Lab in the World!"

Cookie blinked her eyes and wagged her tail and did a little doggy dance, but she was careful when she gave her kisses. And she was very careful when she wagged her tail. And she never, ever, stole a sock again.

A CHRISTMAS CAROL
by: Walt Zientek

The old man started to grumble out loud. "Damn shoppers!" he growled to himself as he tried fruitlessly to find a parking space in the crowded mall lot. Pushing his tired body through the crowd, he finally made his way into the store. He was assaulted by twinkling, blinking lights, canned holiday music, plastic holly and garish garland.

"Merry Christmas!" shouted a beaming, pimple-faced clerk. The man just scowled. "Happy Holidays!" called a chubby cashier in a ridiculous Santa hat. The man just stared and paid his bill, shoved his change into a front pocket and "harumphed" as he risked life and limb, trying to return to his car.

After a plain meal, the man settled into a battered chair and let his body and mind calm down as he sipped a sweet, red wine. The heat from the ancient woodstove felt soft against his face as he drifted slowly to sleep...

"Here Duke!" he heard a child's voice call from far away. "What?" he wondered in his sleepy state. "C'mon Duke ole boy," he heard again. Closer. He opened his eyes and saw a familiar youngster standing next to a powerful black lab. The boy and dog didn't seem to notice him in his old chair in that barren living room.

The boy knelt next to the dog and put his arms around his neck, hugging gently, yet firmly. "I love you Duke," the boy whispered without embarrassment or shame.

"C'mon Big Guy, Mom's calling and supper's ready! Let's go." The old man watched through half opened eyes as the two figures strode away and seemed to fade away.

He let the warmth of the fire lull him back to sleep.

"Hi Honey!" he heard a sweet feminine voice call to him. "Merry Christmas!" it said with much excitement. He slowly opened one eye, just enough to see a beautiful woman in an old-fashioned dress and hairstyle, stand up on her tiptoes and throw her arms around a strong, handsome young man. The man beamed back at the woman, wrapped her in his powerful arms and swung her around. "Merry Christmas, Baby!" he replied in kind as he held the woman until their images began to fade from the old man's sight.

"Santa has been here!" he heard the child's voice exclaim. "I must have been a good girl this year!" she shouted as she ran around the brightly decorated tree. The big yellow dog followed merrily behind, its fat tail clapping happily against the lower branches.

Through his damp and barely opened eyes, the old man watched the child and her dog explore the wonder of a Christmas morning. He watched them as she opened all her simple gifts and showed them proudly to her friend. The big dog sniffed each one politely and seemed to smile at his owner's glee.

The man blinked to try to clear his eyes. Each time he did, the little girl and her dog seemed to blur a little more, until finally, they were gone.

The man sat up in the old chair and rubbed his face with his dry, chapped hands and slowly pushed himself to his feet. He ignored the cold from the used-up stove and found his way to the kitchen and the phone that hung there on the wall. He dialed a number from a memory he had thought he'd lost.

"Hello?" a woman's voice said on the other end.

"Hello?" it repeated.

"Merry Christmas, Honey," the old man barely whispered.

"Merry Christmas."

"What?.... Who?" the woman asked softly.

"Merry Christmas, Honey," the man said in a steady voice.

"Merry Christmas. It's your Dad."

ON CHRISTMAS MORNING
by: Walt Zientek

(Remembering Joshua and Zachary)

On Christmas Morning...

...I wish, for every dog searching trash cans for breakfast, a filled bowl with his name printed in bright letters.

For every dog that slept fitfully last night, chained in a frozen yard, a soft, warm bed with a person snoring gently nearby.

For every shelter dog, spending Christmas morning in a soiled run, a forever home filled with sounds and smells of family.

For every "Christmas" pup given today, a tolerant, caring owner who won't abandon you as you grow into a real dog.

For every ailing pet, enough money for your owner to pay the bills to make you well.

For every lost dog, a clear, safe road and well marked path to lead you home.

For every old and tired friend, a warm fire and soft bed to ease your aches and pains.

For every Heart Dog at the Bridge, a moment when you know that you are remembered today, missed again and loved forever.

ZACHARY'S SONG:
A STORY IN A STORY ... IN A STORY
by Walt Zientek

"OWNER ALLERGIC," the classified ad read, "LAB PUPS, YELLOW MALE, CHOCOLATE FEMALE, UNRELATED, $200.00 EACH".

The man sat at his keyboard and easily remembered that day so long ago, when his daughters were three and five years old. When Joshua was gone, the yard empty. When the thought of a family growing up without a dog, was impossible.

I made a phone call and listened to a sad story about itchy eyes and deep regrets and special prices and took a ride over, after work that day.

He thought about a yellow Lab to fill the space his Golden left behind. He recalled thinking that maybe the house would stay a little cleaner. That maybe the dog would be a little calmer. That maybe it would be enough like Josh to make him happy and different enough to keep him from getting sad.

"I was met at the door by the chubbiest, wiggliest, attention-seekingest Chocolate girl I had ever seen. With her was a woman who seemed to turn on her allergies as we spoke."

He wondered about the yellow male. What was he called? What did he look like? Was he a Velcro dog as well? The man remembered all his thoughts clearly.

"She went out back to let him in. I couldn't help but notice the pure white Maltese sitting on a pillow on the sofa near her spot, or the old striped cat sleeping on the chair."

The man remembered being sure, the moment he saw the pup. A little leggy and lean and obviously not a future champion or a show dog. Too long backed and tall. And a tail-and-a-half! But still the man was sure.

"I asked about his name and learned he'd never had one. Five months old, three months on the porch without a name. He'd never seen a collar or a lead or been wormed or vaccinated. He seldom felt a human touch."

The man paused in his writing. He remembered the sadness and suspicion he felt. He remembered as well just how sure he was.

"I borrowed some money and brought him home. My wife held him on her lap in the car. The girls peeked over the seat and the pup, of course, peeked back. We tossed around a bunch of names but none felt right until I offered 'Zachary'. It was 'Zachary' for the next thirteen years."

The man found himself smiling at that memory. He liked the strong Old Testament names. The kind the rugged pioneers had used. Images of solid men of strength and hope and wisdom. He reached down and scratched Caleb on the head.

"I carried little Zachary up the front steps. He didn't know what to make of them. Within days he was flying up and down the stairs, that incredible tail wagging and slapping against every wall and doorframe. And every night he took his place beside our bed."

The man stretched out his long legs and let his mind float free. He remembered carrying that pup. He also remembered when the pup grew old, carrying him again. When icy steps challenged old, unsteady legs. He remembered too, how he had to gently wake the old boy when it was time for bed. How he'd give him time to stretch and shake away the cobwebs then help him up the stairs. He remembered bandaging the happy tail so many times.

"Zachary grew up to be all I'd ever hoped for, and much, much more. Our family was his life and our home, his world. He loved everyone, but would subtly place himself between the girls and someone strange. He never hunted, but would retrieve a ball or toy all day, and when a flock of ducks flew overhead he would stop and watch, as if remembering something from another time.

He'd suffer anything the girls would do. He'd lie down on the floor and let the cats climb over him. He'd ignore an open gate. Even when his hearing failed, he watched my hands for silent commands. He never messed or destroyed or begged or bothered. He was Zachary. Nothing more, nothing less. Just a good boy. I miss him."

The man stopped his story here. He had a million tales more to tell, praises to sing, events to recall. He wanted to write all of the ordinary things that are the stuff of memories that help define our lives.

He wanted badly to pay tribute and say thank you and

hoped that somehow, somewhere the big guy would hear and understand. He wanted all these things and more.

But he had to end his story there, because his eyes and heart were truly full. He realized that in no small way each piece he wrote would be because of Zach. He realized that in this way he could finally really write, "Zachary's Song."

A DAY AT THE BEACH
by Walt Zientek

"Hey Caleb!" the man called out, "Do you want to go for a ride? Do you want to go to the beach?"

The big yellow dog froze dead in his tracks, cocked his head, gave the man his best "I just won the Lottery!" look and bolted to the closet where the leashes were kept.

He could barely control his excitement as he waited for the man to don his sweater, jacket, gloves and hat, protection from the February cold. The dog did multiple Lab Loops around the room and then really tried to sit while the lead was attached.

The man used the drive time to think and to talk to the dog. The dog used the time to pace relentlessly back and forth in the rear of the SUV, to jump from window to window, to make some really silly dog noises and to prove that patience is a virtue two-year-old Labs do not possess.

"This drive would be a lot more fun if you'd just lie down and stop smearing up all the windows," the man complained.

The dog of course, just redoubled his efforts.

After perhaps the world's longest thirty-five minute drive, the two arrived at the east coast beach with an ancient Native American name. Two or three minutes of wrestling got the safety rigging disconnected and the long woven lead attached. The pair jogged really, really fast out onto the seemingly endless stretch of sand.

"O.K. fella," the man said softly. "It looks pretty deserted. You can run now."

With the snap of the release clip, the big yellow dog was

off, running the water's edge, kicking up the sand, splashing through the icy water. With the snap of the release clip, the dog was free to be a dog.

The dog really played that day. He chased the sticks and the gulls, smelled the sea and tasted the salt and shed the constraints of the civilized world. The man played that day as well. He ran and called and chased and laughed and threw the sticks. He too shed the stress of the civilized world.

The two best friends played for hours that frosted February day until the wind and cold reclaimed the shoreline. Until the sun began to set. Until they both knew it was time to go.

"The beach is pretty cool Big Guy," the man said out loud as they both stared, through watery eyes, out over the ocean.

The man used the drive time home to think and to talk to the dog. The dog used the time to curl up on a thick wool blanket and dream dreams about seagulls and sticks. And the sea.

Another Birthday Song

ANOTHER BIRTHDAY SONG
by Walt Zientek

Sang 'Happy Birthday' to my dog today. Two years old already. He didn't like my voice much. Or maybe he loved it. What's it mean when they jump straight up and butt-tuck around the coffee table with their fur all up and a glazed look in their eyes and then try to run out the back door? Must be some primitive pack-behavior thing. Couldn't be my singing.

Thought a lot about the dog birthdays and how many times I've sung that song. Saw some photos from 1974, with a damned smart Golden named Joshua that had a heck of a first birthday party that year. Boy I miss that big guy. Miss a lot of the folks that were there, too. Sang that song to him, ten times.

Sang to Zachary too. Thirteen times. He would look at me with wise Labrador eyes and smile. Hey, you all know that Labs can smile. He was way too calm to get all worked up about a little singing. He just grinned and brought me a toy. All big occasions needed to be honored with a toy in mouth. My daughters sang to him as well;

their little girl voices went on to become soft woman voices that could carry a tune even when he couldn't hear it anymore. Zach wore those silly hats with great pride and silence. Can't even tell you what I'd give to sing that song to him a few more times.

So today, for Caleb on his second birthday, I sang that song again. I hope to sing it many, many more times.
Happy Birthday Caleb Tucker,
Happy Birthday to you.
Dad

A Boy & His Dogs

A BOY AND HIS DOGS
by Walt Zientek

"A Boy and His Dogs." He looked at the words and let his mind roll back some forty years, to a tiny, faded memory of a small black dog.

"Midnight," he thought, amazed that he even remembered a dog that 'ran away', so long ago. He remembered a very little boy standing in the back yard calling and calling. But not much more.

The face of another small black dog leapt into his mind. He recalled his Mom asking if he wanted a puppy. One that someone rescued from being drowned.

'Lady' came home and stayed for more than ten years. She watched and guarded over the neighborhood kids until the day she died. He remembered her baby-sitting his brother and himself until they left for school. And how she'd walk next door and spend the day keeping an eye on the smaller kids and how she'd chase away the stray dogs, no matter the size, that dared to venture too near.

He remembered the day they drove Lady to the Vet's for

the final time. Waiting in the car while his Dad worked out the details. He remembered talking to her but he couldn't remember what he said, only what he felt.

For several years, he was busy doing the things that young men do and didn't have a dog in his life. But one day his beautiful bride brought home a Golden Retriever he named Joshua, and he hasn't been without a dog since then.

He and Josh were so alike. Big and strong and a little headstrong as well. A perfect match for that time in his life. But as the man grew up Josh grew older. His big, wonderful heart gave up one day. He waited to say good-bye to his family and then closed his eyes.

'Zachary'. He would always hold Zach in his heart and his memory. The boy was now a family man and Zach was the dog that his children would always recall as the family dog. Quiet, well behaved and smart. As gentle a dog as ever lived. Perfect for that time in his life.

He owed a lot to Zachary, and for years to come he'd pay tribute to him in words and deeds. He missed him every day. Zachary will forever be his private Lab.

He remembered a drive not too long ago to visit a kennel. Three yellow male Labs in a litter of nine, only two-weeks old. Caleb would be one of those boys. In three weeks, he and his wife went back again to make a choice. He had planned a very careful test and evaluation. He would be quite sure.

One fat, smiling puppy pushed his way through the crowd and threw himself into his wife's arms and covered her face with kisses. He tried to be objective. He picked him up and turned him over and set him down. He watched him move. When he tried to talk the pup barked once as if to say, "Hey, look at me!" The pup jumped back into the man's arms and into his life and his heart. Caleb chose them.

He thought more about the words, 'A boy and his dogs.' About the almost magical way he'd owned the dogs he needed for the times in his life. He thought the true beauty of a boy and his dogs was that they would live forever in his mind. Even when the boy had become a man.

THE ODYSSEY
by Walt Zientek

He was frightened. And cold. And lost and desperate to get home. The sounds from the road were a nightmare of noise. The fumes assaulted him. They burned his nose and confused him.

His pads were sore. His legs tired and weak. He longed for his bed and bowl. Home was becoming a fading memory of warmth and happiness.

His collar chafed. The rough weeds scratched and jabbed at him. Twilight brought a sudden chill of rain down on his head.

Too tired to walk. No place to sleep ......

"Come on Buddy! Let's go! Time to eat! It's getting dark and it's starting to drizzle. You're getting to be such a BIG BOY! Maybe next time we can walk all the way around the block!"

FROM A DOG GUIDE
by Walt Zientek

"What color am I?"
I'm the color of the streets we walk safely together.
Of granite steps and rough brick paths.
  I'm the color of the wind that touches, coolly, on your
cheek, and the sun that warms your face on summer days.
  I am the color of the nights we spend, just you and
  I alone. The color of the stars that watch us from afar.
  "What color am I?"
I'm the color of a child's voice at play.
Or of a lover's touch, and gentle simple words of trust.
I'm the color of the freedom, blessed in your life and the
bravery in your heart and in your hopes. I am the color of
the soul we share together, just you and I alone. The color
of the years we walk together.

COME VISIT AGAIN
by: John Arrington

Tweet-tweet. Tweet-tweet. Tweet-tweet. The yellow pup raised her head, wheeled in the direction of the sound, and accelerated to full speed. Ahead she could see him standing and searching the dunes for a glimpse of her. She exploded from the cover of the dune grass and raced towards him. He saw the blur of yellow fur, smiled and tooted the whistle again. The pup bounded across the beach towards him. When she was about five yards away he raised his hand and blew a single blast. The dog lifted her head, dropped her butt, dug her feet into the sand and skidded to a stop in front of him. "Good girl," he said and handed her half of a small dog biscuit. She gazed intently into his eyes and remained motionless until he released her with an OK.

It was the kind of day he relished. The world outside his parka was almost entirely gray. It was cold and stormy and the wind driven rain stung his face. The wet sand, the ominous sky and the forbidding ocean were defined by differing shades of gray. Formations of gray-brown pelicans soared on the wind, peeled off and dove into the icy water in search of a meal. Only the foamy white surf, the dune grass, and the yellow pup were not gray. The pup explored the driftwood maze at the edge of the dunes, discovering and investigating the abundant and unfamiliar scents. She was a beautiful yellow Lab, barely six months old. She moved with grace and the athleticism born of youth and good breeding; it was difficult to take his eyes off her.

In deference to a bad back, he walked at the ocean's

edge where the sand was hard. As he walked, he remembered other wet and windy beaches and another Lab, a big yellow dog he called Cheddar. He'd lost her to old age almost 7 months ago. He no longer mourned her loss. Instead he relished his recollections of good times shared for nearly 16 years. On days like this her presence was nearly palpable. It was as if she were there at his side, enjoying the day and the antics of the yellow pup he'd named Chamois.

He often indulged in the fantasy that Cheddar was there with him and he talked with her. He didn't believe in ghosts. It was just a feeling he had sometimes that she was there watching and helping him with the pup. "She's a lot like you, you know. She does that lonely sad thing with her eyes when I leave her behind. Bet you taught her that! And I know you taught her how to lean her head in the crook of my arm and stare at me when I'm driving. And how to catch popcorn with her mouth."

The weather was changing. The sky was mottled with gray and white and blue. Out on the ocean a dark rain-squall moved on the wind. He watched it for a moment then shifted his thoughts to the yellow pup. She was nowhere to be seen. He knew she was close at hand, but just to make sure he put the whistle to his lips. Tweet-tweet. Tweet-tweet. Tweet-tweet. His eyes scanned the dunes ahead of him. Nothing! He turned and looked behind him. Tweet-tweet. Tweet-tweet. Tweet-tweet. Again, nothing. Without warning the pup crashed into the back of his legs at high speed nearly taking him down. "Cheddar must have taught you that too, damn it!" he grinned.

The old man and the puppy turned and headed for home. The puppy bounded from scent to scent. She found an important stick, dropped her prize at his feet, and wagged her tail proudly. He looked down and smiled. Goose bumps covered his body. It was the way Cheddar had told him she wanted to retrieve. In the same instant, the sun emerged and a rainbow suddenly bridged the space between the churning ocean and the sky. "Come visit again," he said to the rainbow. Drops of rain decorated his cheeks ... and diluted a single tear.

THE WATCH DOG
by: John Arrington

They went to the beach this morning. To a little sheltered cove on Humboldt Bay where he used to take me to swim and retrieve sticks and bumpers. John doesn't know it, but I've been sent back to watch out for them. It was a picture book day with a blue sky and big white puffy clouds. The air was crisp and cool and smelled of salt water, seaweed, and wood smoke. It was Chamois' first experience with a beach and a lot of water. It took them almost ten minutes just to get from John's truck down to the water's edge. I used to cover that ground in less than thirty seconds. But you have to understand, Chamois isn't even 15 weeks old yet and she's still learning what kinda stuff is good to sniff and what she can ignore.

When they got down to the water, John let Chamois off the leash. I could tell he was nervous about that. I mean she's still kind of ignorant about stuff, but I wasn't worried. She's a Lab like me and I knew she'd do just fine. It didn't take her long to figure out she could run to her heart's content on a beach. No fences to stop her here and before they'd gone 50 yards she was doing that silly puppy butt tuck thing and was hauling buns in big circles around John as he walked along the shore. Chamois wasn't interested in getting her feet wet yet.

About the same time I saw him, John and Chamois saw him too, a big yellow Lab boy running down the beach towards them. I could tell this guy was cool, but John guarded Chamois closely during the sniffing ritual. He always looked out for me that way too. Big Yellow wasn't wearing a collar and he was soaking wet. After the greet-ings, he wandered off looking for a stick. Chamois stuck close to John and when Big Yellow was a safe distance away, she started butt tucking again. Big Yellow found a good stick and I told him if he wanted John to throw it for him to sneak up and drop it on his foot. That's what I always did. It worked for Big Yellow too. The three of them walked down the beach together. John threw the stick in the water for Big Yellow and Chamois barked at Big Yellow when he brought it back.

I was always good at reading John's thoughts and he hasn't changed any since I came back here to help him with Chamois. He was worried about introducing her to the water. And this walk at the water's edge was the same way he'd gotten me wet the first time. Of course, I was older and went right in the minute I saw it. And I knew he was thinking about all those times we went to the beach together. Throwing the stick for Big Yellow brought a lot of those memories back for both of us. His arm's kinda outta stick throwing shape through 'cuz I was too lame the last few years for swimming and retrieving in cold water.

I could see that Chamois just wasn't going in the water without a little help from me and Big Yellow, so I got into her head a little and whispered, "That stick could be yours, don't let Big Yellow have all the fun." It worked like a charm. John tossed the stick for Big Yellow and Chamois took off after him. It was perfect! She took a couple of big leaps just as a wave came in and before you could say 'Science Diet' she was in deep water and swimming. She turned towards shore and paddled her little butt off and came bounding out of the water like an old veteran. I haven't seen John so excited in a long, long time. He was saying, "Good Dog, Good Dog, Good Dog," and I heard his voice quiver with excitement. "Good Dog, Good Dog, Chamois, you were swimming. Good Dog!" he was so proud of her. Me too ... 'cuz now she's a real water dog like me.

Chamois didn't go back in again and John didn't push it. A few minutes later they turned and headed back towards the truck. On the way home, Chamois put her head in his lap and went to sleep. I still feel kinda funny about that, you know, John letting her put her head in my favorite place. I know it makes him feel good and it makes him remember me so I guess I don't mind. But I wonder how long it will be before he stops getting those tears in his eyes when she puts her head in his lap? I miss him too.

THE POSE

by: John Arrington

The sun was warm on my back as I crunched along through the soft sand on the shore of Big Lagoon. A big sand bar littered with driftwood protects the calm water of the lagoon from the crashing Pacific surf. Across the sparkling water, about two miles away, the ragged silhouettes of giant Redwoods marked the opposite shore. Cormorants, ducks and shore birds of various shapes were the only creatures sharing the afternoon with us. Chamois, my 15-week-old yellow Lab, was busy sniffing and exploring and bounding from one new scent to the next, unaware I suppose, of the serenity and beauty in which we were immersed.

When I loaded Chamois into the truck that afternoon, I was hoping to get her to swim. The night before she'd gotten over her initial reluctance to trot along in ankle deep water and seemed to my eager eyes to be ready for the big plunge. She'd actually swum a few days ago when she chased Big Yellow into deep water, but that was an "accidental" swim. I was looking for a volunteer. She didn't seem afraid of the water, just not very interested.

As we made our way down the beach, Chamois alternated between sniffing all in her path with sudden butt tucking scampers with a stick in her mouth. On several occasions she came to screeching halts at my feet and dared me to try and take the stick from her. When I ignored her, she'd drop the stick and dig a hole in the back of it and then offer it to me again.

"SIT," I said and to my astonishment she did. "GIVE," and she let me have her prize. When I tossed it in the water she gingerly waded out to it, pawed at it and managed, somehow, to push it to the bottom with her foot. You could see the wheels turning in her tiny head. "Where did it go? If it's gone, I'm gonna go sniff some more stuff," and away she'd go. This scenario was repeated again and again. A tiny armada of once treasured and now forgotten sticks floated on the water behind us.

Then it happened. A flight of brown pelicans came swooping in over the sand bar and like a formation of jets on a strafing run they dived down, leveled, and glided over the water without so much as a single flap of their wings. I turned to see if Chamois had seen them. She had. She was standing at the water's edge in one of those perfect poses you see the handlers trying to achieve with their dogs in the show ring. Left foot back, tail straight as an arrow and raised ever so slightly from horizontal, ears perked forward, head held high and alert, her back as level as the horizon, and she was absolutely motionless. Her "pose" was perfect in and of itself, but in that setting with the deep blue sky, wind rippled water, sand, trees, and a dozen or more pelicans in the background, it was breathtaking. I stood there slack jaws for a moment, before I realized it was the photograph of a lifetime. I fumbled for the camera hanging from my neck, pointed it toward Chamois, but before I could release the shutter she turned and trotted towards me. The magic vanished as quickly as it had materialized.

On the way home, Chamois slept soundly with her head in my lap ... completely butt-tuckered out! My mind returned again and again, as I drove, to the mental image of Chamois' great pose at the water's edge. It was a prizewinner, a magazine cover shot. If only I'd been an instant quicker with the camera. Or maybe it's better this way ... my vision of The Pose is sure to improve with age.

THE WATCH DOG,
THE OLD MAN, AND THE PUPPY
by: John Arrington

CHEDDAR: They went to the beach again this morning. It was foggy and cold. Chamois doesn't know it yet, but she'll be going to the beach a lot on foggy days. John says fog keeps the tourists away and he can have the beach to himself. And that's how it was this morning. I was there too, but since I've come back to help John with Chamois, I'm invisible. I don't mind as long as I'm not forgotten.

JOHN: As we walk along, I can't help but think of all the foggy beach days I enjoyed with Cheddar, my Labrabuddy for almost 16 years. This new pup is different. She is bold where Cheddar was timid and timid where Cheddar was bold. And unlike her predecessor, challenges me on nearly everything. But she's beginning to come around and starting to know what to do without a lot of instructions. Sometimes she responds to new stuff as if she already knows what I want.

CHEDDAR: Of course she does, John. She's a Lab and has me to help her. But she IS a little pistol and, as far as the beach goes, she doesn't even know yet that eating crab shells can be a pain in the butt tomorrow. But she'll learn and John keeps her out of big trouble like he did with me. She's lucky you know ... to have such a soft touch for a partner. He can get really mad if you do something you know you shouldn't, but after he scolds you there are always hugs and pats on the head and he talks softly in your ear and asks if you can be buddies again. And when you wag your tail and give him your biggest saddest I'm-ever-so-sorry Lab eyes, he'll even give you a treat.

CHAMOIS: Yeeeehawwww. Look at me. I can run so fast it makes my ears fly. Nothing can stop me. I can run for-ever out here. Watch this turn. Now for the brakes. Wow, that really makes the sand fly. This is a blast! What's that smell? And this one? And this other one? Sniff. Sniff. Sniff. I'll run right past him, make a hard right and do a couple of circles. Yeeeeehaaa! Brakes. BRAKES. Look! An old shirt buried in the sand. I'm gonna pull it out and run with it. Tug. Tug. Tug. Yeeeehaawwww. I'm gonna run with it.

CHEDDAR: Stupid kid is gonna trip! Better tell her to drop it and ... too late. Nice form on the forward roll though, I gotta admit. Now shake off all that wet sand kid. That's right.

JOHN: Boy, I love this kinda day. Listen. It's so quiet. Chamois, that's the sound a cormorant makes with its wings when it takes off from the water. And there, can you hear the fog horns on the jetty and the clanging bell on the channel buoy? LEAVE IT! CHAMOIS, LEAVE IT!

CHAMOIS: Now why is he always saying LEAVE IT? This thing smells great. Wonder what it tastes like. Yuck! He's calling me again. Hey John, watch me run. Wonder how fast I can go. Wow, this so cool! I'm gonna try some zigs and zags. Yippee. There's John. Here I come, full speed ahead! BRAKES! Yikes ... Looook oooout!

CHEDDAR: On the way home, Chamois fell asleep with her head in his lap. John's getting better about this. No tears in his eyes today when he looked down at her and remembered me. Today, he smiled and stroked the soft puppy fur on top of her head and I heard him think, "Well, Chamois, you're gonna be all right. When we get home I'll wash that sand off with the hose. Cheddar always liked that." Don't believe him kid. He'll hose you down with cold water and if you don't hold still and let him get all the sand off when he dries you with the big blue towel, that sand on your belly will rub you like sandpaper. So hold still and pretend you like it.

BEAU AND THE 12-HEADED MONSTER
by: John Arrington

The bike riders are clad in black Lycra shorts and tightly fitting jerseys decorated with a riot of color. They ride in a disciplined pace line. Sweat glistens on skinny forearms and bulging quadriceps. They talk and joke and laugh as they ride. It is just past 6:00 A.M. on a warm July Sunday morning.

A mile ahead at the top of a short steep rise is Beau's yard. Beau is a heavyset, sinister-looking black Labrador Retriever. Beau protects his yard and his family with unswerving diligence and a loud chorus of barking whenever strangers approach. If the threat is especially menacing, Beau supplements his barking with a swift hard charge that invariably sends the intruder packing. This morning Beau is stationed in his usual place under the porch. It is shady and cool there and he can see all the territory he must defend.

The riders slow as they ascend the hill that leads to Beau's yard. As they labor against gravity, the only sound is the whir of the freewheels and the whoosh of hard exhalations.

Beau sees the riders as they crest the hill. He has seen bike riders before and takes pride in chasing them from his territory. But this is something new. A dozen riders moving as one. To Beau it is a 12-headed monster with 24 arms and 24 legs. He has to protect his family. He has to be brave. He explodes from his hiding place under the porch and charges across the yard, hackles raised, fangs bared, barking his fiercest bark.

The riders are taken by surprise. It isn't the first time they've been attacked by an unrestrained dog. They usually avoid a confrontation by out-running the beast. But this dog is unusually fast and is very nearly upon them. It is too late to run for it. The riders reach for the only anti-dog weapons they have, water bottles and tire pumps.

When Beau reaches the edge of his yard he hesitates for a moment. He isn't supposed to go out of the yard and the street is definitely off limits. But this is a 12-headed monster with 48 appendages. There is no telling what it will do to his family. He has no choice. He has to break the rules and he clears the sidewalk and the curb with one great leap.

Among the riders is a man who has a Lab a lot like Beau. Instead of reaching for a water bottle or tire pump, he looks at Beau and says, "Hey, where's your ball? Where's your ball?"

A few minutes later one of the riders said, "Man, I couldn't believe it. He just stopped and went looking for a ball. It was amazing. How did you know he had a ball?"

"He's a Lab. Labs are nuts about tennis balls. I had a friend once who swore he was going to name his next Lab "Wilson" so all his tennis balls would have his name on them."

The riders laughed and then fell silent. The only sound was the whir of the freewheels and the whoosh of hard exhalations.

Beau is back in his favorite spot under the porch. He has a soggy green tennis ball in his mouth. If the 12-headed monster with 48 appendages comes back, he's ready.

Beau + the 12-headed monster

OF MICE...AND MEN?
by: Walt Zientek

Okay, first ya gotta get a historical perspective on all this. About 500 million years ago, people had this primordial thing in their brains that made the men "hunters" and the women "gathers." The men took off every morning to wrestle down a mastodon or a saber-toothed tiger, and the women gathered up a few roots and berries while they mostly complained about their men, drank coffee and wished Victoria's Secret would get invented.

Well, in my family tree, some distant relative with an underdeveloped "hunting gland," decided that this tiger-wrestling thing was a losing proposition and he volunteered instead to "guard" the women. It seems he had some other, more 'highly' developed glands that were suited for better things.

From that point on, about the only things the men in this family have hunted have been some clean underwear to wear to work, a tie to wear to the bowling banquet and a place to find some peace and quiet.

(Segue now to the present day)

"I think there's a MOUSE in the kitchen!" I hear my wife say in a stage whisper.

I pretend I don't hear. Of course, that never works.

She tiptoes out to the living room with a look of terror on her face.

"Go see!" she commands as she gets up on the sofa and pulls her feet securely under herself.

"SIGH!" I exclaim as I make my way.

My two good-for-nothing cats are acting like something is under the cabinets.

"Go earn your keep!" I tell them as I open the cupboard doors.

They rush in and I go back to the TV. But not for long.

"SIGH!" I exclaim even louder as I am chased back into the hunt. Seems the wife doesn't CARE about my illustrious family history. Apparently, that "gathering gland" is still active in her line, as is her expectation about a "man's job." SIGH.

Well, the cats are having a ball, knocking stuff over and squeezing in behind the dishwasher and chasing each other. All the commotion finally wakes the dogs and they stumble into the kitchen.

"Aha!" I think. One 100-pound Lab, with a natural hunting instinct and one French Bulldog with a noble, "ratting" history.

They make a beeline to the far right cupboard. The one where the food is kept. And the treats. And the chew bones.

"Get the mouse!" I command in my strongest voice.

The lab runs to the toy box and the Frenchie grabs a pig ear. So much for all the help.

"Did you catch it?" I hear from the other room.

"Catch it?" I think. I'm supposed to "catch" it? Four natural hunters won't "catch it", but I am supposed to. SIGH.

A trip to the hardware store yields enough traps to endanger the entire species. Peanut butter, hard cheese, soft cheese; a regular rodent buffet is prepared. Several fingers are damaged but still I press on. I make enough noise placing the traps to scare the mice back out into the winter cold. Always hopeful.

I begin to feel that primitive gland growing in my brain.

Soon, I am mapping out my trap lines. I begin to think like a mouse. I start to desire "camo" clothing. I am really getting into this.

I must be giving off pheromones like crazy, because the wife is sure looking at me differently as the "hunter" emerges from beneath the cabinets.

"SNAP!" I hear. "SNAP!" again. Success! The mighty hunter has prevailed and the world settles into its correct balance. I head back to the TV.

Apparently, the "gathering" gland excludes "gathering" up the dead mice and I am sent back under the sink. Yuck.

With much chest-puffing and self-confident smirking, I present the vanquished quarry.

"Ahhhhhh!" is all I hear as she runs screaming from the room.

"You 'squished' the poor little things!" she says.

My smirk disappears.

"You killed them," she whimpers sadly.

My chest deflates.

"Go WASH your hands!" she orders.

I feel my "gland" shrivel. SIGH.

THE BIG BREAKOUT
by: John Arrington

It was one of those hot summer evenings. The air was still and quiet. It was nearly dark. A cloud of dust followed my truck into the driveway. Even before I got around to the front of my house I sensed that something was wrong. It was too quiet. No excited greeting from the two Labs, Swamp and Bubba, who'd been left behind in the house for most of the afternoon. When they were quiet, it usually meant I was about to encounter a scene of mayhem and destruction inside the house. As I rounded the corner, the screen door caught my eye. The heavily reinforced portion at the bottom was twisted and bent and pushed out from the inside. Opening the screen revealed broken glass and chunks of wood with huge teeth marks. The dogs had broken out of the house by chewing their way through the wood that held the panes of glass in the French door and had then wrought havoc on the screen to escape.

I was worried. They'd eaten their way through the door. My first thought was that some neighborhood kids had come into the yard and had harassed the dogs thinking they were safely locked inside. Or maybe a burglar had been lurking and the dogs had called his bluff. Not knowing the answer, I started searching for the dogs, half expecting to find blood and gore and the dismembered parts of children or burglars strewn about the premises.

I wasn't thinking clearly. After all, these were Labs I'd raised from pups and knew them well. They were the big sissies who hid under the bed on the 4th of July. What could possibly aggravate them enough to break out of the house and maybe attack a stranger? If the burglar came while I was gone my chief worry, heretofore, was that they might lick him until he giggled to death. However, the apparent violence of the dogs' escape suggested something sinister to my worried mind.

The house next door was vacant, the victim of a bitterly contested divorce. A perfect place for an injured intruder to hole up. So I began my timid search there. Maybe it was just vandals my dogs had attacked. I circled the house looking for signs of damage, forced entry or worse. As I came to the backyard I heard something behind the 6fi-foot high board fence that surrounded the swimming pool. I froze in my tracks, held my breath, and listened intently. Yes, there it was again. The unmistakable sound of breathing. With my heart pounding and my hand quivering, I checked the gate. It was securely latched. I found a chlorine jug crate, dragged it to the fence and used it as a stool so I could see over the fence. As I climbed up on the crate and stood on my tiptoes, I held my breath. Would there be a severely wounded and dangerous intruder inside? Perhaps a small frightened child covered with blood and barely conscious. What would make my dogs injure or maybe even kill someone? They were such nice dogs. Whatever it was, I was sure it was bad!

I peered over the fence and there in the middle of the pool were Swamp and Bubba, calmly and literally swimming laps. How they got over that fence, I'll never know, but it sure took determination and one helluva strong desire to go for a swim. I was so relieved to see them safe and sound and still the gentle sweet dogs I'd left behind that afternoon, they got big hugs instead of a scolding.

BUBBA SPEAKS
by: John Arrington

Do you remember those talking dolls? You know the ones that were popular in the mid-seventies? The dolls had a little round plastic ring attached to a string that hung out of their back. When you pulled the string it activated a voice box inside the doll. The doll had a vocabulary of 5 or 6 phrases like "My name is Kathy," or "I'm hungry," or "I'm sleepy."

At the time, I had a black Lab named Bubba. Bubba was just over a year old. He was big and clumsy and chewed on everything. I should have named him Beaver! One afternoon, the kids from next door were in our yard throwing a tennis ball for Bubba. Retrieving tennis balls was the only thing Bubba liked better than chewing. About ten minutes after the kids went home, Bubba walked into the kitchen. He had one of those little plastic rings from a talking doll hanging from his mouth. The metal voice box was clenched between his teeth. I reached down, pulled the string, and Bubba said, 'I Love You!'

Bubba spit the voice box out and began barking. His hackles were up. He charged the tiny metal box and retreated again and again. I collapsed on the floor and laughed until my stomach hurt. The next day, I bought the kids next door another doll. It was a small price to pay to hear my dog say, 'I Love You.'

THE WORLD CHAMPION STINK DOG
by: John Arrington

Swamp might seem an unusual name for a dog, but those who knew her understood its origin. From her perspective if it was wet or stinky, it was simply fabulous. Swamp was neighborhood famous for lying in mud puddles and swimming in anything deep enough for paddling. However, Swamp earned her name by rolling in dead birds, dead fish, horse manure, cow pies, moldering garbage, and other aromatic delights. No other Labrador Retriever in history was shampooed and deodorized as regularly and as frequently as Swamp. How she entirely avoided skunks was an unfathomable mystery.

The day she acquired the title of World Champion, we were walking on Bastendorf Beach near Coos Bay on the rugged Oregon coast. It was November and the steel gray sky spit drizzle mixed with rain. The wind from the stormy Pacific was raw and cold. The broad expanse of beach was deserted. Even the sea gulls hunkered down on the sand and refused to fly unless provoked. We were the only ones brave enough or foolish enough to be out in the weather. Swamp, oblivious to the storm, trotted from scent to scent exploring and discovering the beach things that fascinate dogs. I, on the other hand, retreated into the warmth and shelter of my parka.

We were old hands at beach walks so I paid no attention and continued walking when she disappeared from view. Five minutes, maybe more, had elapsed before I noted her absence. I knew she wouldn't stray; nevertheless, alarm signals sounded. I began calling and whistling for Swamp.

She did not respond. What had become of her, I wondered, and what has she gotten into now? It took another five minutes of backtracking to find where her paw prints turned away from the shoreline. The tracks led into a maze of driftwood logs and hillocks of sand topped by clumps of yellow-green dune grass.

My nostrils quivered and I raised my head and sniffed the air. Yes, there it was, the unmistakable odor of decomposing flesh. Swamp had found something dead and would be rolling in it when I found her. She would stink; I would have to give her a bath. It was nothing new or unusual. After all, her name was Swamp.

The stench of death grew stronger and drew me inevitably toward a ghastly scene. Swamp had found the decomposing remains of a long dead sea lion. She was covered from the tip of her tail to her eyebrows in a thick gelatinous goo that resembled Vaseline. The slimy goo, the bones and the head were all that remained of the creature. Up close, the aroma was nauseating. The rain and the wind were forgotten. Goo removal became our prime directive.

The only thing Swamp loved more than rolling in stinky things was retrieving. That trait would be our salvation. I picked up a stick of driftwood and walked toward the water's edge. Swamp followed. I threw the stick into the surf and she charged after it. Again and again she leaped into the churning water to retrieve the stick. Gradually the goo was washed away. When most of the slime was gone, we headed back to the truck and home. It was bath time ... big time!

Weeks and gallons of deodorizing shampoo and exotic concoctions finally conquered the malodorous 'Eau de Sea

Lion', but not without a struggle. The stench adhered to everything. Friends and neighbors avoided us. A rumor circulated that a cat tried to buy my truck. It was untrue!

Swamp was my first Lab and my inveterate companion for thirteen years. I still miss her cheery disposition, and happy thump of her tail, and even the faint scent of something stinky that seemed so much a part of her. Yes, Swamp was truly the undisputed World Champion Stink Dog.

World Champion Stink Dog

THANKSGIVING DINNER
by: John Arrington

Now you've got to understand my mother to really appreciate this story. Mom is a fastidious housekeeper. Obsessive compulsive might be a more accurate description. A single example will illustrate her absolute dedication to an immaculate household. Once I came home from college for a visit and no sooner was I in the door than I was offered a glass of milk and a plate of my favorite homemade sugar cookies. I sat down in front of the TV and before I'd eaten the first cookie, mom was busy with her little carpet sweeper making sure that if a crumb had fallen on the rug it wouldn't stay there for more than five or six seconds.

OK, now imagine her distress when I showed up for Thanksgiving with two big black Labs. "You aren't going to bring those dogs in the house are you?" she asked as the dogs burst into her living room dragging me along behind them. She suggested they might like to stay in the garage for the entire weekend. I suggested they'd freeze their buns off because they were used to living in sunny San Diego and this was Boise and there was snow on the ground. After some negotiations and pig- headedness on my part, a compromise was reached. One dog at a time in the house during the day and both dogs could stay inside at night as long as they were confined to my room. Thanksgiving dinner came off without a hitch and mom seemed to be getting along just fine with the dogs. She even petted Swamp a couple of times but Bubba, the boisterous 1fi year old, was just too much for her.

The day after Thanksgiving, my sister and the dogs piled into my truck and we drove up in the mountains for a day of cross-country skiing. When we returned, Bubba went in the garage and the rest of us went inside. About fifteen minutes later, we decided that a hot turkey sandwich was just the thing to restore our spirits and hold off the hunger pangs until dinnertime.

"Mom, where's the turkey?"

"I put it out in the garage ... there wasn't room in the refrigerator."

Tracy and I looked at each other and made a beeline for the backdoor that opened into the garage. Bubba was standing over the roasting pan licking his chops and there was nothing left of the leftovers except a nude turkey carcass. I mean NOTHING was left. Not a speck of stuffing nor a scrap of meat. Bubba ate it all. Thankfully the major bones were still present, but if we had waited another fifteen minutes the bones might have been consumed too.

When I broke the news to Mom, she was incredulous. "I put it on that little table. I didn't think he could reach it there." The table in question was not quite as tall as a standard dining table. And Bubba was the same dog that ate his way through a door and scaled a 6fi-foot high fence just to go for a swim.

For the next couple of days, I was really in the doghouse and Bubba's poop was gaily festooned with shiny bright aluminum foil.

THE MATING GAME
by: Walt Zientek

I'm sitting home this Saturday,
(Wishing all the rain away,)
When in my mail, I should read,
Dian's post on "How to Breed!"

It seems to get the breeding true,
You 'teach' the male what to do,
Commands are used! He gets it right!
(Forget the sweet romantic night.)

The male hasn't got a chance,
(No flowers, wine or slow, close dance.)
Bring him over, point the way,
"Get it done or go away!"

Nothing now is left to fate,
(even how the doggies mate)
Give a signal, clap your hands,
It's all, "Slam Bam, thank ya ma'am."

While reading this, (You know us Guys,)
We see the metaphor's disguise.
And recognize the "breeder's tale"
Is intended for the human male!

You want to take the fun away,
Eliminate the way we "play".
Blame the hormones that we make.
Claim it is a big mistake.

Sorry ladies, you won't win,
Not the "mating game' we're in.
We'll never let you run our lives!......

But first, we'll have to ask our wives.

A BREEDER'S PRAYER
by: Walt Zientek

Please let me be prepared enough,
To handle any emergency or crisis.
Please let me be lucky enough,
To have a healthy Momma here to hug.
Please let me be blessed enough,
To hold many fat and healthy babies in my hands.
And finally, Dear Lord,
If you decide this isn't meant to be ...
Please let me be strong enough,
To cope with heartbreak, tragedy and grief.
Amen.

PICK OF THE LITTER
by: Walt Zientek

Research. Research. You've read every book from Nichols to Howe, from New Skete to Pryor. You've devoured all the magazines, journals, digests and quarterlies. You have surfed the Web, scoured the stacks, and scoped the specialties.

You've queried, questioned, interrogated and e-mailed dozens of breeders. You have studied pedigrees to seven generations, doubled checked on clearances and then checked again.

You know more about genetics than most biologists. You are boring your friends. Your spouse will barely speak to you. And still you research.

Your phone bill is longer than the U.S. Constitution, including the Amendments. You can identify kennel prefixes from 20 states and 4 provinces. You know bloodlines from England, New Zealand, Scotland and the Philippines. And still you research.

Finally, the day arrives. You and the breeder have accepted each other. You have studied temperament tests. You are armed with whistles, balls, feathers and a 27-point check-list.

You take a deep breath as you enter the whelping room. 12 puppy eyes look up at you, but two lock on tighter than a missile guidance system. One fuzzy pup pushes through the pack and takes a leap of pure faith, right into your arms.

Kisses, puppy breath and an unspoken agreement about respect and unconditional love are exchanged at that moment. A bond is formed.

So much for research ... you've become the pick of the litter.

TOUCHING MEDIOCRITY
by: Walt Zientek

She sat at one end of the sofa and placed her hand on the hip of the old sleeping dog. She smiled as she remembered the first show they'd entered. She recalled how the nicer folks there commented on her good points as well as gently pointing out her faults.

She also recalled how other, not as nice folks, made a face and moved away. Her hand lightly stroked the dark yellow fur as she remembered how her hopes were never met in the Ring. The dog was fixed and took the role of pet to heart. She'd always be a mediocre show dog. That really didn't matter anymore.

* * *

His right hand lifted the steaming coffee to his lips as his left draped over the brown dog's back. The frosted autumn morning was silent, still and young. He talked quietly to the big brown dog as they waited together in that old blind. He talked of things he'd never say with other folks around.

The big dog listened well to every word. He knew the ducks were not around that day and really didn't care. He wasn't eager to swim the icy pond or fight a crippled bird, but of course he would. If his master's aim should magically turn true, he'd do the job. For him.

* * *

She knelt down and lightly squeezed the black cheeks between her palms. She wondered if this goofy boy would ever understand the exercise. She shook her head and laughed as he just seemed to grin and hang his tongue.

* * *

The man stood silently beneath the big tree. His eyes were locked upon the marker on the ground. His minded raced through the memories. He allowed his heart to speak, to cry and mourn. He placed his hand upon the stone and held it there a long, long time. He felt a cold nose touch his arm, a wet tongue against his skin. The gangly pup nudged and pressed his head against the man. The man hugged the pup and held him closely for a little while, before they turned and walked away.

PLEASE SIT WITH ME
by: Walt Zientek
(For Amy)

Please sit with me tonight
and gently lie your hands upon my face.
And smile
And tell again the stories of my youth.
And laugh
And bring out tender memories of a time
that seems so long ago.
Please sit with me tonight
and bring my family near so I can see.
And talk
And say those silly names again.
And sing
And share again the joyous songs
that filled our home with love.
Please sit with me tonight
and gently lie your hands upon my side.
And understand
And feel the words that come up from my heart.
And say good-bye....
And guide me as I take the journey to my final home.

THE BLACK DOG
ALLEGORY – A PROLOGUE
by: Walt Zientek

He was beautiful. Easily the most handsome pup in the litter.

An ebony beacon across a sea of gold, coat shining pure black and radiant.

Yet no one noticed him.

He carried bloodlines for courage, heart, desire and drive.

His potential was unlimited, unhindered.

Yet, he was unwanted.

He was short coupled. He had substance, structure and bone.

He was balanced without compromise to fad or fancy.

Yet, he was overlooked.

He was under priced. Under valued.

And because he was what he was, people feared him or

crossed the street when they saw him. Even those who should have known better tensed, or turned to other things and other dogs.

Lesser dogs pulled down the prizes, fame and fees. Lesser dogs were pampered. He lived a life of solitude and loneliness. Because of this, he barked at people passing by. He barked to find a friend to toss a ball ... or say a kind word. He barked, not to frighten, but to beckon.

The Black Dog's story is one of waste and loss. One of ignorance and foolishness. One of trends and styles and whims and bias and frustration, difficult to imagine, impossible to condone.

So, one day, in an effort not so much to get away, but rather to get to something better, the Black Dog broke his chains.

THE BLACK DOG ALLEGORY – FREEDOM?
by: Walt Zientek

He was free. For the first time ever in his life. Free of chains and boredom and neglect. Free to test his legs and his heart. Free to learn about the world. Free to run the mean streets.

He brought gentleness, intelligence and a longing for respect and love. He found cruelty and ignorance, hunger and thirst and for the first time ever, he felt pain and tasted blood.

He fought the feral urban packs for dirty, spoiled, scraps of food. He felt the senseless cruelty of man. He learned to bite and steal. He learned to hide, fight and cry.

He was forced to use his intelligence to survive. He learned to dodge the city's cars and trucks. And where a meal might be found. And where a restless sleep was safe.

The Black Dog's story became one of pain and hardship. Of brutality and survival. One of lost ideals and dreams. And prayers that went unanswered. More than real, less than fair.

Until, one day, in an alley where he fed on bits of trash, the Black Dog saw the Man.

THE BLACK DOG ALLEGORY – THE MAN
by: Walt Zientek

He was standing. The man was standing against the wall.
The Black Dog picked up the human scent long before he
saw him there. Standing still and smiling.

His clothes were heavy, old and soiled. Worn.
He was neither young nor old, but his eyes were wise and
warm. And he smiled.

The Black Dog circled carefully, eyes averted, tail down.
He fought against the things he'd learned, the lessons of
the streets that pulled against his once gentle nature. His
need for love.

And because he was what he was, he moved closer.
Carefully closing a gap far wider than those few yards.
Trying one last time to fill a dream that only dogs can
dream.

Lesser dogs would run or growl or bite or merely shy
away. Lesser dogs would remember all the cruelties they'd
felt. And not forgive.
Or not remember why they broke their chains and ran.
What they were searching for.

The man put out his hand. And touched the dog.
Touched his head and touched his heart. And with that
simple gesture, touched his soul.

THE BLACK DOG ALLEGORY - EPILOGUE
by: Walt Zientek

They still walk. The Black Dog and the Man, still walk those city streets. Together. As they make their way through life. No one notices them.

They have never become rich. Or famous. Or powerful. They make their way quietly. Giving what the other really needs.

Going to Water

GOING TO WATER
by: Walt Zientek

The dog was waiting by the door,
And so we went with bumpers in hand,
Across the field that was nearby,
To where the water meets the land.

Not needing any excuse to go,
Because the summer's air was warm,
(Well, hot) you see the sun was high,
No clouds or rain or chance of storm.

We ran as if the water called
Our names aloud that golden day,
And ancient longings pulled us forth
As though this was much more than play.

But once along the shore we paused,
Like children lost in silent awe,
And said a simple quiet prayer,
For crystal waters that we saw.
Each stopped and stared just straight ahead,

And smelled the softness in the air,
And forced ourselves to wait a bit,
Before the pleasure we would share.

When our restraint could hold no more,
(Most surely you could understand),
We threw ourselves into the pond,
And chose the water, over land.

THE PUPPY AND THE OLD PRO
by: John Arrington

She stood erect, head held high and proud, nose to the wind. Her yellow coat was wet and matted. Muddy water dripped from her belly. Just 16 weeks old and already looking like an old pro.

He watched and remembered another wet yellow dog with her gray muzzle held high and proud. Her coat wet and matted. Muddy water dripping from her belly. She was an old pro.

Like the puppy and the old pro, he held his head high and proud.

Tears of sorrow diluted by tears of joy trickled down his cheek, and soaked his gray beard. Muddy paw prints decorated his trousers.

THE PERFECT RETRIEVE
by: John Arrington

The gray in his beard notwithstanding, he was as green as his pup when it came to retriever training. After several weeks of attending the retriever club's weekend training sessions, he'd worked his way up from spectator to bumper thrower. This weekend they'd entrusted him with a hand held two-way radio, a blank pistol, a clutch of bumpers, and a folding chair. His job was to yell, "Hup hup hup hup", shoot the pistol and throw the bumper high in the air and across the ditch in front of him.

Being a bumper thrower involved a lot more standing around waiting than it did throwing. It was a lot like playing softball in the 5th grade. Because he couldn't throw straight and couldn't catch worth a darn, he was the 5th grade's permanent right fielder. Being the permanent right fielder involved a lot of standing around and waiting ... but you didn't get a chair.

Across the intensely green pasture, a caravan of pickups, vans and SUV's were parked along a fencerow. Each vehicle contained kennel crates and Labs or Goldens and bumpers, and all the other paraphernalia so familiar to people who love Retrievers. Small knots of people wearing rubber boots and "camo" jackets leaned on fenders and talked about dogs. They all had whistles dangling from lanyards strung around their necks. They watched one dog after another run various combinations of marked retrieves. In one of the trucks, a dog barked and yelped demanding its turn to participate.

A woman with a pretty fox red Golden Retriever named

Mac emerged from behind a huge dark green Ford 4x4 pick-up and approached "the line". Mac was excited and doing spinners but quickly settled down and sat at her side.

The two-way radio buzzed. "John, this will be a single on you." The man in the pasture with gray in his beard stood ready with a bumper and the blank pistol. The woman raised her left hand. John yelled, threw the bumper in a high arc and fired the pistol. Mac streaked across the lush pasture. He hit the water in the ditch with a great splash and climbed the opposite bank where he paused for a moment and shook the water from his coat. He spotted the bumper, raced towards it and without breaking stride scooped it off the ground, wheeled, and sped back towards his owner.

The radio buzzed again. "OK John, come on in and we'll try a few with Chamois." He collected the remaining bumpers, folded the chair and began to worry. Chamois was just a nine-month-old pup and all the other dogs had at least two or three years of intensive field training under their belts. Some were working on their Master Hunt Test skills. Chamois had been through a basic obedience class and had done well, he thought, but this was different. She was retrieving in the back yard, but it was small and fenced and familiar. What would happen out here? Would she even go out after the bumper? What if she wouldn't bring it back? Would she leap into a ditch filled with cold muddy water? These and a hundred other doubts filled his thoughts.

He led the yellow Lab pup to "the line". His heart was pounding. His palms were sweating. How would this pup he loved so much do? He wanted the assembled onlookers to think well of his dog. A man wearing hip boots and "camo" jacket stood near the edge of a ditch. Chamois watched the bumper that hung from his hand. Camo Man yelled "Hup hup hup hup", and threw the bumper high in the air. It landed on the other side of the ditch and maybe 20 yards away from "the line". John released the excited pup and she fairly flew across the ground. "Maybe she'll do it," he thought, "but she's gotta get across that ditch." The yellow blur didn't even hesitate and leaped into the ditch and swam across. Once up on the other side, she searched for the bumper, found it and started back.

"She's gonna do it, she's gonna do it," he said to himself. "She looks as good as Mac. It's not as far, but look at her go! He tweeted the recall signal on his whistle and yelled, "Come on Chamois, good girl." His voice quavered with excitement. "This is great. It's gonna be perfect," he thought.

Chamois ran to the edge of the ditch, down the bank and entered the water cautiously. She climbed up and out and headed straight back towards her human. She was fairly prancing and appeared to be immensely pleased with herself. "Look at me," her body language seemed to say, "look at me, I'm a Labrador Retriever and this is what we do." The knots of people quit leaning on fenders and craned their necks to watch the stylish pup.

Suddenly, Chamois stopped. She dropped the bumper and sniffed at the ground. "What's she doing," the man with the gray beard wondered. "Oh no!" His heart sank. The knots of people leaned on the fenders again and quit craning their necks. Chamois was eating a cow pie!

YELLOW DOGS AND DAYS OF GLORY
by: John Arrington

It was raining hard. The old man was standing in a soggy pasture. An 8-month-old yellow Lab pup named Chamois sat at his side. There were people scattered about the pasture. Each one had a big plastic bucket filled with dead pigeons and ducks. They'd throw a bird in the air and yell "hup hup hup". A Golden Retriever or a Lab would race across the pasture, swim across the little pond, retrieve the bird and race back to the owner. The old man wondered about these dogs. They were so different than his pup. It was as if they'd spent the morning drinking high-octane espressos and eating white sugar. They ran so fast! The dogs were doing all kinds of fancy stuff like being handled to a blind retrieve with hand and whistle signals. He marveled at their skill and wondered if he could ever teach the eager pup at his side to perform similarly.

After everyone had a turn, they asked him if he wanted to "run his dog"? They would set up a simple bumper retrieve. He was reluctant. He'd just come to watch and to see if this was something he wanted to try. Their dogs were so good and this pup had only recently showed enthusiasm for retrieving. What if she just ran around like an idiot? What would they think of his pride and joy? A "showdog" that couldn't retrieve? Beautiful but stupid? An owner who messed up a promising pup? He was filled with doubts. They persuaded him to let his dog try a couple of simple retrieves. A man they called a "gunner" would stand about 20 yards away and toss a bumper. The old man was instructed to release his pup while the bumper was still in the air.

His hands were wet and numb. He struggled to unhook the leash from the wiggling pup's collar. She was quivering, suddenly alert and focused on the Gunner. He was amazed at the instant transformation. She was pulling at the collar and making little squeaky sounds. It was as if she knew it was her turn to retrieve as if she'd done all this before. Her excitement made him think of Cheddar. He often had an eerie feeling that Cheddar was watching and helping the new pup learn to be a Lab. That great old dog had been his companion for nearly 16 years. He missed her. Was she here today helping his pup? He hoped so.

"Hup, hup, hup," the Gunner shouted and twirled the bumper by its rope handle and threw it high in the air.

Chamois raced across the wet soggy pasture. He'd never seen her run so fast. Why she looked just like those other dogs. A chill ran up and down his spine. A rooster tail of spray kicked up behind the flying pup. She ran straight to the bumper. The old man's heart raced. Would she bring it back? Things started to fall apart. She picked it up but ran towards the Gunner. The old man called her name, clapped his hands and moved backwards and away from her. Finally she understood and ran back towards him carrying the bumper by the rope. She pranced and danced and shook her head and tossed the bumper to and fro. "Chamois! Come. Good dog. Chamois come," he said. When the frolicking pup was about ten feet away she dropped the bumper and ran to him and did a nice sit directly in front. He reached into his pocket and pulled out a little dog biscuit. She accepted the treat and his lavish praise with a wildly wagging tail. Not bad for a raw pup's first "formal" retrieve, he thought. The gunner and the others seemed to agree. He was very proud.

In the afternoon, the old man settled into his favorite chair. The yellow pup was clean and dry and sleeping on a big round dog bed next to the chair. Her legs kicked and she moaned and made little chirping sounds. Did she dream of carrying a large wet duck in her mouth while swimming across the pond in the pasture? He closed his eyes and imagined a blur of yellow streaking across a field. He blew a single blast on his whistle. The dog stopped and faced him. He signaled with his right hand and shouted, "Over". The dog moved smartly in the new direction. He blew his whistle again and the dog stopped. "Back," he shouted. The dog wheeled and ran at high speed towards the duck hidden in thick cover on the other side of a ditch filled with water and reeds. A flying leap, a big splash and the dog was across the ditch. She sniffed the ground and her nose led her to the duck. She gripped it gently in her mouth and heard the tweet-tweet, tweet-tweet of his whistle. She raced back across the field and delivered the duck to his hand from a perfect heel position. He smiled and patted his Master Hunter on the head. "Good girl," he said, "Good girl."

The old man and the yellow pup snored in two-part harmony. She dreamed of wet feathers and a "Good Girl". He dreamed of yellow dogs and days of glory.

A DREAM OF GENIE
by: Walt Zientek

So, I had this Genie dream. You all know the one where Mr. Everyman, (me), is walking along a deserted beach with his Lab. Suddenly, the dog starts digging and uncovers an obviously enchanted lamp.

Knowing of course what is expected, I eagerly rub the lamp. Suddenly, after an enormous puff of brightly colored smoke rises from the lamp, a shockingly beautiful and shockingly clad female Genie appears. (She looks suspiciously like a younger and more voluptuous Barbara Eden.)

"I will grant you ONE wish, Big Boy," she tells me.

"Hey, I thought I got three!" I replied.

"You read too much," was her retort.

"What will it be, a couple million bucks, power, your own kingdom?" she asked.

"How about changing some dog stuff?" I asked.

She sort of looked at me funny.

"What kind of Dog Stuff?" she asked. "You want some bones or something?"

"Competition." I told her.

"So, you want to win a dog competition?"

"No." I said. "I want to eliminate all competition between dogs."

The Genie looked puzzled as she ran a perfectly manicured hand through the lushest blond hair I had ever seen.

"Take your eyes off of my navel and explain this fiasco to me!" she commanded.

"Here's my idea," I said as I struggled to make eye contact. "I would like to have dogs judged against the standard, not against each other. Take Labs, for example. Any Lab with all approved clearances could be judged by a panel of three, against the standard. The judges would explain their evaluation to the owner, the only person allowed to handle the dog. The evaluation would include a test of the instinctive retrieve. One judge would toss an object and the dog should react like a Lab, and go after it. This would indicate that the dog had the instinct and with the correct time and training, could be trained to hunt.

Only healthy dogs, with correct temperaments, basic instincts and proper clearances could get the word "Champion" before their names. Only dogs with the title "Champion" could be bred and have their progeny registered. No points. No Majors. No profit in breeding for Puppy Mills. Registration would indicate quality.

"I see," said the Genie. "But what about Field Trials?" she asked.

"For those who really want to train for field work," I replied, "they would first have to get their "Champion" title. This way, only good representatives of the Standard could compete. And then they compete against the course, not against each other. You pass or you fail."

"So, under this system," the Genie said, "Show dogs have retrieving ability and Field dogs all meet the Standard. And, registration and breeding are left to solid examples of the Breed. Boy, are you going to tick-off a lot of people!"

"Yep," I said. "Can you do it?"

"Yes Master" she said. (I really loved that part!)

So the Genie snapped her fingers and blinked her eyes and when the smoke cleared ...

I found myself walking across my old college campus, totally naked, looking for the room where my final exam was being held, realizing that I hadn't attended class for the whole semester.

I guess that's the trouble with dreams. You just never know what you're going to get.

ARE CERTAIN COLORS OF LABS SMARTER?
by: Walt Zientek

The answer to this, of course, is yes, no, and maybe. The rationales are based on science, history, prejudice, tradition and probably some superstition. While all Labs certainly go back to common ancestors, blacks were the predominant as well as the dominant color. A famous quote said, "Labrador Retrievers come in three colors, Black, Black, and Black!"

This attitude, intentionally and accidentally, produced very many "smart" black Labradors over many generations of breeding. It "proved", by default, that blacks were indeed the smartest.

As the yellow Labrador increased in popularity, the momentum began to swing in their direction. A wider gene pool and some excellent breedings by some dedicated breeders, brought the quality level of the yellow Lab up to par with the black Lab. On the other hand, over-popularity produced poorly bred examples of both colors. So the world now had a broad spectrum of Labrador Retrievers in two colors, some great, some mediocre, and some poor.

"Quality" gaps widened even further with the expanding split in the type between "Field Bred" and "Conformation Bred" lines. Besides color bias, form and function attributes had changed between the two groups. Recently, there seems to be an effort at reconciliation between the two camps, but until that occurs the definition of "smart" may not be the same for both groups.

Now the chocolate Lab gets its turn. The cycle is repeating itself. Because coat color was the only criteria in some early breedings, chocolates were not considered the best. As breeders got smarter and breedings got better, the quality of the chocolate Lab has improved immeasurably. Now, however, with the popularity of the chocolates, there will undoubtedly be over- breeding of some inferior dogs.

Is there an "inherent weakness" in any color Labrador? Absolutely not. Dedicated breeding and careful buying will ensure that. By some measures, Labradors of all colors are considered the sixth most intelligent breed. If they look at the true functions of the Lab and at the diverse jobs it does, there are only one or two other breeds that can even compare.

The smartest Lab that ever lived is the one that picked you to love. You don't need an IQ test. You don't need a color chart.

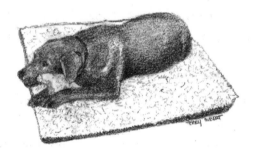

PET SHOP GIRL
by: Walt Zientek

I just needed a few things.

I really didn't need to walk to the back of the shop where the puppies are kept. I certainly didn't need to see one room filled with black and chocolate Labs. I didn't need to have that beautiful black female pup look up at me with those dark, soft eyes.

I suppose I didn't have to kneel down to get as close to her as I did. Or touch the glass and talk to her. Or try to get her tail wagging. I surely didn't need that feeling in the pit of my stomach, the one that makes you think about reaching for your wallet.

I didn't want to think about the place she came from. I didn't want those pictures in my mind. I never wanted to think about the cages and the stink and the dogs being bred, litter after litter until they lost their value as puppy manufacturers. I didn't want to think about her momma in a crate, cramped and dirty and lonely. And sad.

I didn't want to consider how young and frightened she was when she was put in a truck to be shipped back east. How terrified she must have been by the separation and the noise, by the smells and by the sounds. I didn't want to wonder if all the siblings in her litter survived the trip.

I didn't like feeling the way the average person feels when they see a puppy in a Pet Shop. I didn't like the impulses I felt. I didn't want to feel like rescuing her. But I felt that too. I understood why people bought their dogs this way. I understood that saving this dog supported the system, paid the "breeder" and the driver and the shop owner and the clerks. I understood that saving this puppy, this soft gentle girl, fed the system I didn't want to think about.

I didn't really need to feel the way I did: sad, angry and guilty. I didn't need to say I'm sorry or good-bye to that soft eyed little girl who pressed her dark nose against the glass to touch my hand, to get my scent, to be close.

I only needed a few things.

But I didn't need them badly enough to buy them there.

SHERMAN AND THE TANK
by: Walt Zientek

She, being a woman, was blessed of course with chromosomally-linked refinement, taste, and endless good sense.

He, being a man, was not.

She, being an artist, had an inherent eye for style, balance, form, and function.

He, being a single guy, living alone, didn't really understand any of that, but figured he probably had it all too.

When she decided after much introspection and soul-searching to add a dog to her life, extensive research began. She subscribed to all the national magazines. She spent countless hours in libraries and bookstores. She attended all-breed shows and matches. She specially studied the breeds in obedience trials. She queried kennel owners, badgered breeders and jawed with judges. She left absolutely no stone unturned.

When she finally decided on a Sheltie as the breed for

her, the quest for the perfect example began. Line after line and title after title were reviewed. Temperament test after temperament test was given. Finally, a balance of beauty and brains arrived when she brought Sherman home. Even his name said strength, intelligence, and form.

When the man decided one day to get a dog, he looked in the newspaper, found a litter of yellow Labs from a Show/Field breeding and went on down. He picked out the biggest, rowdiest, goofiest guy in the litter. He brought him home, set him down in the snow, and watched him plow his way through the fresh powder.

"Just like a tank!" he thought. And "Tank" it was.

As with all good stories, the woman and the man became husband and wife and by default, Sherman and the Tank became stepbrothers.

While Sherman practiced his obedience jumps, Tank practiced his sofa leaping. While the Sheltie returned the dumbbells to hand, the Lab returned shoes to the cobbler. While the smaller dog excelled in perfect, long down-stays, the bigger dog excelled in long, lazy naps on the bed.

To the man's credit, he tried obedience. Once. But when Tank kissed all the posts and tried to wiggle into the judge's arms, the man decided obedience wasn't really his sport.

To the woman's credit, she tried obedience. Often. And while the Sheltie's perfect form would bring the crowd, cheering, to its feet, the Lab's unbridled enthusiasm would leave them rolling on the floor, laughing.

To everyone's credit, Tank went on to earn his CD and two legs toward a CDX. But his heart and true talent lie in the field, where he has earned a Junior Hunter title. And Sherman continues to seek his "High in Trial" awards in the obedience ring.

And the man? Well, because he is a man, he thanks everyone sincerely when they compliment him on his two well-trained and titled dogs.

And the woman? Well, because she understands her man as well as she understands her dogs, just nods her head and smiles.

CHAMOIS' NOSE KNOWS NO'S
by: John Arrington

So there we were again. It's 4:30 A.M. Chamois is raising hell in her crate and serenading me with all manner of puppy yelps, whines, barks, pleading moans, and agonizing death cries. After seven weeks of these early morning exercises, I've got the routine down to a science. Throw back the covers, roll to a sitting position, mutter an obscenity, slip on the sweat pants strategically located beside the bed, mutter another more colorful obscenity, pull on the slipper socks that were under the sweat pants, shuffle over to the bathroom to relieve the hydraulic pressure, turn on the light, flinch from the glare of a 100 watt bulb and repeat the first obscenity, shuffle to Chamois' crate, fumble with the latch, open the door, get out of the way 'cuz she comes out like a rocket and chases the cat down the hall, etc. You've heard some of this before.

This morning she stepped out of the crate slowly, stretched like a big dog and went for the shoes. Now I'm not into shoes like Imelda or some ladies I know, but I do have more than one pair. And I hate to keep them in the closet 'cuz it's a pain in the lower back to find them when I need them. It's dark in there. So I line up the shoes I wear frequently along the wall opposite my bed and directly in front of the crate. This morning the line up included a pair of hiking boots, a pair of fuzzy slippers, three pairs of old Nikes, and a pair of Birkenstocks. That's a total of twelve shoes. Chamois stuck her nose in the first one. NO! Stuck her nose in the second one. No! Stuck her nose in the third one. No! and so on down the line. Just as fast as I said NO!

to one shoe, Chamois stuck her nose in the next one. Twelve times in a row: "NO! No! No! No! No! No! No! No! No! No! No! No!" until she reached the end of the line and the doorway to the hall. By this time I was laughing so hard I almost forgot to get out of the way of her charge down the hallway after the cat.

Dawn Patrol

APPLE PIE AND THE DOOFUS DOG

by: John Arrington

The aroma of fresh baked apple pie yanked my head around like a Halti collar stops a charging Lab. I coulda' got whiplash. Next thing I know we're headed for home with a hot pie Mrs. Appleseed would be proud of. Chamois, my yellow Labrador Retriever, was droolin' all over the car seat. My mouth was watering too. We were out all morning in the rain and wind. A big bowl of chili, warm corn tortillas, and a huge hunk of pie were exactly what my cold, hungry body craved.

After lunch, I put the pie plate on the floor for Chamois to lick and settled in to watch the NASCAR race on TV. Jeff Gordon was leading. I'm a big Jeff fan. About an hour later I sensed Chamois was not in her favorite place beside my chair. Ohmigod, she got out, was my first panicky thought. I found her sitting in front of the pie plate giving me just about the dirtiest look a Lab can give a human. Two long threads of drool extended from the corners of her mouth to a slimy puddle big enough to float my neighbor's duck boat. The pie plate was as yet unlicked.

I'm sorry, but stifling my roar of laughter was just not feasible. I slumped to the floor and laughed 'til my sides ached. Chamois didn't move an inch. She just drooled and gave me dirty looks. No matter how hard I laughed she remained solid as a rock. I did not wet myself, but it was a near thing! Only the timely application of manual pressure prevented a pants wetting catastrophe

What's so funny about a drooling dog? I'll explain.

I once read a dog-training book written by some Monk

guys. The Monks are big on the idea that dogs should be religious too. They teach us that religion is instilled in dogs by enforcing a sit command for a while before the dog eats. This "quiet period" allows the dog time to meditate and give thanks to the AAFCO (American Association of Feed Control Officials) for the complete and balanced nutrition it is about to receive.

Or was the waiting period one of those "leader of the pack" Alpha dog deals? I don't remember for sure.

Whatever! Chamois has to wait until I say, "OK," before she eats. So she'd sat there for over an hour waiting for me to say, "OK." Unfortunately, I was laughing too hard to say it. I'd squeak out maybe half of a syllable of "O" and she'd shift her eyes to me and then immediately back to the pie plate. Her brow would wrinkle and she'd twitch her tail a couple of times and then look back at me. That would cause still more fits of irrepressible laughter. I swear I nearly passed out from oxygen debt. Eventually I was just too tired to laugh any more. It must have taken a minute or more before I could gasp out, "OK," and Chamois could finally lick the plate clean.

For obedience above and beyond the call of duty, Chamois got a big bite of Tillamook Cheddar and a sliver of pie. For dereliction of duty and unforgivable delay with the release command, I was summarily demoted from Alpha to Doofus dog.

THE POOP TEST
by: John Arrington

When inquiring about the acquisition of a puppy, I was not surprised to discover that the best breeders had as many questions about me as I did about them. Fair enough, I got a great puppy and puppy got a great home.

However, after coping with Chamois for five weeks it is evident that questions asked by breeders do not identify persons mentally and physically qualified for raising a Lab puppy. In order to remedy this sorry state of affairs, I propose that the AKC and LRC and NAHRA adopt and standardize the Puppy Owner Optimization Program Tests (POOP Tests). The Poop Tests would seek to simulate in the ring situations commonly encountered by owners of Labrador Retriever puppies aged 7 weeks to 1 year.

Individuals who successfully complete the tests will be recognized as "qualified to cope" and authorized to affix the initials QC after the name when signing a breeder's puppy contract. The names of individuals who fail the tests will be logged into a national computer data base and classified as having "POOPed Out". No stigma shall accompany this designation and individuals so designated shall not be disqualified from attempting to qualify at a later date. POOPed Out individuals will be provided with information about Lab Rescue organizations and encouraged to adopt an adult dog.

I shall propose the first of these tests and trust that others on the Lab-L list will contribute other tests based on their own Lab puppy raising experience.

Test #1: Bitter Apple Quick Draw! Barefooted contestant is seated in a recliner in the full tilt position, eyes closed to simulate snoozing. There is an end table next to the recliner with a spray bottle of Bitter Apple. A signal is given. Contestant brings recliner to full upright position, grabs the Bitter Apple and sprints 20 feet through an obstacle course consisting of items placed randomly between the contestant and the goal line. The obstacles shall consist of 6 tennis balls, 2 Nylabones, a medium Kong, a tennis shoe, a 1 liter soda bottle, 2 rubber squeaky toys, a floor lamp lying on its side, and the confetti of an issue of Dog Fancy. When the obstacle course has been completed, the contestant stops at the goal line and sprays Bitter Apple at a 6-inch bulls eye target 2 feet beyond the line until he or she hits the mark. A passing score is achieved if the contestant can complete 10 repetitions of the procedure in a combined aggregate time of two minutes or less. Not more than 30 seconds shall be allowed between the completion of one run and the next.

When we have a representative body of tests and have agreed on their efficacy, I say, "Let the POOPing begin." So come on, let's hear from you!

BARITONE OR SOPRANO?
by: John Arrington

One of the great pleasures in my life is listening to music via my high-end stereo. My audiophile buddies would call it a "listening system". At the end of a long or stress filled day, I select a favorite jazz album, fire up the system, open a cold one, and settle into the luxurious comfort of my green leather recliner. Ahhh, peace and quiet and mellow music.

That's exactly what I was doing the other day when Chamois, my 15-week old yellow Lab pup, started pestering me. Knowing that in a few more weeks she'll be too large to be a lap dog, I lifted her into my lap and managed to calm her down so I could enjoy the music and my beer. The soothing music of Bill Evans washed over us and in a matter of minutes we were both snoozin'.

Did I tell you I have a cat? She's a beautiful calico. She wandered into my life one day, skinny, neglected, stray, and frightened. I'm a soft touch when it comes to pitiful looking critters. The cat was welcomed, spayed and became a part of my life. She doesn't do much besides eat and sleep, so I named her Doolittle. When Chamois joined us, Doolittle was not pleased. This puppy wanted to chase her and play. Doolittle wanted to eat and sleep. At first Doolittle kept her distance from the pup but has learned somehow that while Chamois may be clumsy and too enthusiastic, she means no harm. Nevertheless, Doolittle maintains a safe distance whenever the pup is near.

Which brings us back to snoozing in the recliner ... no that's wrong ... I was waking up ... because my nose was twitching and tickling and there was something heavy on my chest. I opened my eyes and all I could see was cat fur. Doolittle was camped out on my chest with her tail just under my nose. My arms were folded across my belly and were the only thing that separated cat and puppy. At this point in the story I'd like to say "and they lived together happily ever after."

However, when I reached to remove the cat tail from under my nose, Chamois woke up, saw the cat just inches away and lifted her head from my lap. That's all it took for all hell to break loose. Doolittle freaked, turned on the afterburners, dug her back claws into my chest to gain enough traction for her opening leap towards the hallway and sprinted towards the safety of her favorite spot on my bed. I winced and said something obscene as the pain message from the ten claw marks on my chest reached my brain. Chamois reacted too and did her version of a flaming burn out with all four paws across the most delicate part of my lap. Wince number two and the resulting profanity and pain message followed number one by a microsecond. By that time, both critters had disappeared down the hallway. I followed at a more genteel rate of speed gripping my wounded chest with one hand and my wounded delicate parts with the other. By the time I got to the bedroom, Doolittle was safe on the bed and Chamois had changed her focus to the laundry basket. She had the biggest mouthful of dirty socks you can imagine.

I sat down on the edge of the bed and called Chamois hoping I could get my socks back without a struggle or a chase. Her ears perked up at the sound of her name and she trotted towards me shaking her head violently from side to side to make sure the socks were good and dead. I extended my hand, said "GOOD DOG, GIVE!" She walked towards me and I was relieved to see she intended to deliver the socks. But her method of delivery wasn't the classic sit and deliver to hand advocated by dog trainers. Instead she jumped towards me and delivered blow number two to the most delicate part of my lap and dropped the socks at my feet. Although it required a supreme effort, I managed to wheeze, "GOOD DOG" before I curled up in the fetal position hurting and wondering if I'm going to emerge from Chamois puppyhood as a baritone or a soprano.

DOG FOOD ... THE DEFINITIVE ANSWER
by: John Arrington

She is such a beautiful pup. She has stolen my heart. I subscribed to the Lists. I read every post and studied the advice, especially the discussions about nutrition and food. I want my girl to grow up strong and healthy. I am determined to feed her the best. But it's all so confusing. What to do? What to buy? I decided to start reading labels because that's what a good consumer is supposed to do, right?

So I bought a little spiral bound note pad and headed for the pet stores and the feed stores and the grocery stores. I read labels and made notes on Eukanuba, and Iams, and Precise, and Science Diet, and Pro Plan, Pedigree, Attaboy, Alpo and about a hundred others. Do you know they put Menadione Dimethylpyrimidinol Bisulfite in dog food? Try and say that one fast ten times ... or just once! I wrote down the ingredients and made comparisons and ended up more confused than educated.

Omega-3 fatty acids. Lamb and Rice (poor little lambs). Vitamin assay per kilogram? Is my precious puppy getting enough Choline? Is 2,800 mg per kilo enough? Minerals, too, are important and what dire consequences will result if 0.04 mg per kilo ("based on calculated values as per laboratory research") isn't enough Selenium to keep my puppy from losing her hair? So many decisions, so little knowledge. And I haven't even begun to analyze the Amino Acid profile (percent of total) yet ... does anyone REALLY know how much Isoluecine, Cystine (thought that was a chapel with a painted ceiling) or Methionine is enough or too much? And should I buy Brand X or Brand Z if one has more Taurine than the other? So many decisions, so many dog foods. And what the heck is Poultry Digest anyway? Poultry Digest sounds to me like short stories for chicken farmers, but the label says it's in Chamois' food. Who knew?

We spent the better part of a weekend doing dog food label comparisons and by Sunday afternoon I was exhausted. Chamois was tired too, so we went to McDonald's and got cheeseburgers and fries!

THE HOUSE WRECKER
by: John Arrington

FOR HIRE: Yellow Lab House Wrecker. Young, enthusiastic, experienced! A specialist in house plan confetti making, magazine shredding, shoe chewing, carpet piddling, furniture gnawing, water bowl dumping, cat annoying, sock stealing, pant leg attacking, leash biting, gate crashing, toilet paper unraveling, TV remote control munching, electric cord biting, table lamp busting, beard pulling, trash can tip-overs, neighbor nibbling, throw rug towing, kitchen towel tugging, house guest harassment, laundry basket scrambling, litter box spilling and most other forms of mayhem. Guaranteed results! Will work like a dog for food. Interested parties contact Chamois, the 10-week-old wonder puppy at Jrington@aol.com.

WISE EYES
by: Walt Zientek

(for Cinder)

The tall man sat back in his chair and stared at the screen. His eyes were fixed on the image of the dog that appeared there. He didn't realize how transfixed he was, until the screensaver snapped on and broke his reverie.

He quickly brought back the image and asked himself why he was so captured by this dog, this particular Lab? Sure she was pretty, but he knew he thought they all were. And she was awfully thin from some very bad times she was going through. No Show queen, this lady, for sure. Just another pet amongst millions. But she was speaking to him through her picture and he was determined to hear what she was saying, for he felt the message was important in some way. He damned his own stupidity and lack of sensitivity.

"Come on girl, whisper to me," he asked the image quietly. As if in answer, he was drawn to her eyes and his heart fluttered a bit. "Wise eyes," he heard himself say. "This little girl has such wise eyes, it is as if she knows something we don't."

Some dogs have soft and gentle eyes that beg you love them. Others have dark and frightening eyes that dare you to even look back. But this dog had Wise Eyes that locked on yours and touched your mind as well as your heart; that could tell you stories if you were careful in how you listened; that made promises about certain truths you needed to believe.

The man let his mind float free as he stared into those eyes and he knew he was hearing some of those thoughts, feeling some of those emotions. Someone had told him that Labs could see into your soul and now he knew how.

Thanks to the little girl with the soft, wise eyes.

THE LOOK
by: Walt Zientek

(For Kylie and Peg)

It is most definitely a "yellow Lab" thing. Perhaps it occurs in other colors or other breeds, but it is surely found in every yellow Lab. They are the masters of "The Look."

Usually, the sweet, sad-eyed expression dominates the countenance of a yellow Lab puppy. The heart warming, innocent look that makes you want to reach out and scoop them up in your arms. The look that gets them belly rubs and way too many treats and toys. This however, is not, "The Look."

"The Look" is something else all together.

If you ever raised a yellow pup, you have seen it. "The Look" can arise just before a wild Butt-Tucking spree. It can strike just before those razor-sharp puppy teeth sink into your forearm. It can happen just before the pup decides to climb upon your dining room table or to eat your reading glasses or to roll in the smelliest, nastiest, filthiest pile of organic matter.

In the time it takes the owner to say, "Uh Oh!" the sweetest most innocent yellow dog can transform itself into the Devil's Spawn, right before your eyes.

"The Look," is hard to describe but easy to recognize. Those soft, dark eyes seem to glaze over, the velvety ears go all crooked and lopsided.

Tiny puppy teeth seem to become glistening needles of destruction and the pup tilts its head, as though listening to a silent command from a dark, unseen, malevolent master.

What happens next is not for us to anticipate or understand. The now-transformed puppy will respond to this command of evil with lightning swiftness and single-minded zeal. Something will break. Some rules will be ignored. The Cosmos will tilt a bit, slightly out of balance, for just a few moments, as the yellow pup completes its task.

And then, as quickly as it starts, "The Look" disappears and the quiet yellow pup returns. It doesn't seem to understand the commotion all around. It is puzzled by the yelling, screaming, crying and moaning. It wonders why the broom or vacuum or paper towels are being used. It wonders why it is getting another bath. It wonders why it is time to go to the crate.

So folks, hug your yellow Labs. Give them treats for doing tricks. Scratch that favorite spot along the neck or on the tummy. Dress them up for special occasions, take their pictures and have parties on their birthdays. Pat their heads and gaze lovingly into their eyes. But be ever vigilant. Watch out for "The Look."

THE CANINE
by: Walt Zientek

Once upon a midnight bleary,
as I sat there drunk and teary,
Reading Quarterlies and Digests,
full of dogges of yore
While I nodded, nearly napping,
suddenly there came a tapping,

As if someone quickly rapping,
rapping on my hardwood floor.
"It's the heat pipes," I muttered,
"tapping on my hardwood floor.
Only this and nothing more."

Ah, foggily, I recall it was a cold and dampish fall
And each separate leaf that fell,
made my mind a living hell.
Eagerly I dreamed of spring.
Rashly I had sought to bring

From my magazines of dogges
longing those that came before,
Nameless here for evermore.

Presently, my head was clearing,
likewise was my suspect hearing,
"Hey," said I. "My head is killing,
show yourself I do implore!"

But the truth is I was napping and
so gently you came tapping,
tapping on my hardwood floor.
That I wasn't sure I heard you.
Quickly I scanned across the floor
Doggy Hair and nothing more.

Thoroughly I checked my room,
in the light and likewise gloom,
In there sat a stately dogge of the saintly days of yore.

Not the slightest whimper made he,
not a timid look he gave me.
But with an air of something royal,
sitting on my hardwood floor.
Sat and looked and nothing more.

There, this magic dogge
beguiling my sad expression into smiling,
By the soft and kind expression on the countenance it wore.
"Though thy coat be short and harsh," I said,
"You've come in from the marsh.
Ghastly, damp and regal Dogge,
wandering from the Nightly Shore.
Tell me what thy lordly name is,
since you've entered through my door."
Quoth the dogge "LABRADOR."

Much I marveled this dogge dear,
to hear the discourse so clear,
Though its answer little meaning,
little relevancy bore
For we cannot help agreeing
that no living human being
Ever yet blessed with seeing
dogge upon his hardwood floor
Dogge or beast upon the polished
wood of his chamber floor,
With such a name as "LABRADOR."

But the canine, sitting, sitting,
lonely on that whining wood,
spoke only that one word,
as if his soul in that one word he did outpour.
Nothing further then he uttered,
not a word was spoken or stuttered.
Till I scarcely muttered,
"Other dogges have gone before!
Come tomorrow you will leave me,
as the ones who came before!"
Then the dogge said, "LABRADOR."

And that canine,
never flitting, still is sitting, still is sitting
On the polished wood of oak
that makes my chamber floor.
And his eyes hold all the dreaming
of a heart that's true, not scheming.

And the firelight, over him streaming,
throws his shadow cross the floor
And my soul from beneath that shadow
that lies floating on the floor,
shall be freed by "LABRADOR!"

THE VET
by: Walt Zientek

She was dog-tired. And cat-tired, too. Three hours of scheduled surgery this morning and four emergencies, all before she even started her regular appointments.

The hot bath water stung the scratches on her arms and hands. She examined the deep, angry slice left by the old, pugnacious tomcat and made a mental note to re-apply antibiotic.

While she tried to physically relax, her mind replayed the events of her day. Every stitch, exam, booster and x-ray. Every worried owner, frightened kitten and goofy puppy. They all returned like a television program playing on a screen behind her eyes.

She felt involuntary tears well up as she recalled an owner's sad good-bye to an old trusted friend. God, she hated that part of the job. But she did it with grace and warmth and tears. Always tears.

She started thinking about money. Her overhead was outrageous and her past due accounts growing. She never refused service for lack of funds. Too many folks were leaving her high and dry.

She stretched her leg out toward the tap and used her foot to add more hot water. It felt good. She squeezed her eyes closed and let her head slip deep beneath the scented water. Her mind released a mental sigh.

* * *

He was worried. His little girl was not acting right. She always had a typical Lab appetite, but she only ate half of her breakfast this morning. When he walked her before he left for work she seemed OK.

When he stopped home at lunch to check, her tail wagged as usual, but she still hadn't finished the food in her bowl. He didn't like that. Still, she seemed to be fine.

After work, she jumped up and acted just like herself. He forgot his worries and headed to the beach to exercise a bit and to give her a little bumper practice. She really did seem fine.

When he put her food down that night, she sniffed and walked away. He felt her nose. Cold. He looked into her eyes and she licked his nose. He wondered if she'd grown tired of her food.

Her whimpers woke the man that night. From her spot at the end of the bed she cried quietly and he bolted awake. Not knowing what was wrong or what else to do, he dialed the Vet's number.

* * *

They met outside the darkened office. He held his little girl and wore a serious worried expression. She held her keys and wore her wet hair pulled back in a ponytail that soaked the fabric of her old faded sweatshirt.

Together they made their way to the exam room. She asked a dozen questions on the way. He answered and apologized but explained that he just didn't want to wait until morning.

Her well-trained hands quickly went over the yellow pup. She checked her heart and her temperature and as she started to check the little girl's throat, the puppy gagged and started to choke.

The Vet reacted instantly and grabbed a corner of the object that had made its way back up, into the puppy's throat. She deftly pulled the soft fabric clear of the Lab's mouth.

The puppy coughed a few times and spit up a little on the table. Then she swallowed, wagged her tail and kissed the Vet across the face.

The Vet and the man stood together beneath the bright light and examined the foreign object. The man looked embarrassed. The Vet shook her head and chuckled quietly as she held up the soggy sock.

"You really, really have to be careful with these things, Mr. Arrington," she said sternly, but with a smile.

The man blushed behind his rough white beard and nodded his head sheepishly in agreement.

"Look at the bright side," the Vet said. "This little girl will make you a much better housekeeper." "I guess she will," the man replied. "I guess she will."

* * *

The man carefully attached the harness and buckled the yellow Lab securely in the passenger seat of the small pick-up truck. He drove slowly and stopped at the front of the office, where the Vet was locking the doors.

"Thank you, Doctor," he said sincerely. "I appreciate it."

"Good night John," she said with a smile. "Good night Chamois."

THE WOMAN'S DAY
by: Walt Zientek

1. The house was finally quiet. The holiday fuss had wound down. Even the dogs decided to nap. The woman took the quiet time to get things put away. Sorted out. She started moving pieces of jewelry from the old, worn box to the new one. Rings and chains and pins and earrings, all with special memories that made her smile. All found a place in the drawers or on the new pegs.

Her fingers touched a shape she couldn't identify. She gently lifted the object from the bottom of the old box. Dog Tags. Not gold or silver or precious stones. She read the lines engraved there. Her fingers read the worn words. Her mind went back to the other times.

She put the tags up near her face and swore that she could still remember the warm familiar scent of the old boy that wore them. She didn't know how long she stood there, clutching those memories so tightly in her hands. She felt her face grow warm as she glanced across the room.

She smiled one more time and placed the tags in a special place within the new box. Her hand rested for a moment on the lid and she wiped her eyes. The box held so much more than jewels.

2. The woman walked outside on that clear, cold winter's night. The dogs seemed to sense her mood and walked quietly around the yard, giving her a little room, not asking her to play.

She gazed up at a sky so perfectly clear and breathed

deeply of the frozen air. She felt a touch of vertigo as the stars seemed to envelop her. Her mind raced with thoughts, questions, fears, dreams, memories, feelings, losses and wonders.

She shivered, but not from the cold.

This was a time when the words she loved so well were simply not enough. There were really no words for what she saw, felt or remembered that night. This was a prayer without a name. A little psalm of the soul that could never be written. A poem without meter or rhyme. An essay without a theme. A dance to a tune that only she could hear, to music only she could feel.

She shivered once again. This time from the cold. In a husky voice she gently called the dogs by name and touched each one softly. She smiled a smile that was joyful and sad and something else. She turned and headed for the house. So many things to do.

3.   She breathed deeply again. This time the steamy, perfumed air filled her lungs as she settled comfortably into the bath. A pair of wise brown eyes were fixed on her. Smiling. She smiled back.

The woman was thankful for this day. Precious and rare. A day with time to think and, most of all, to feel. A day to put demands aside. Indulge the spirit. Renew the body and the soul.

She took her time this night. Holding on a bit, stretching time as best she could. Moving slowly.

Eventually, she made her way to bed. The dogs jumped up and claimed their favorite spots and settled in. She touched each one and listened to them sigh. With comfort.

In the pleasure of that so familiar.

She shut the light and listened for a while more.
  She didn't hear herself sigh.

HEALERS
by: Walt Zientek

"Here is a picture," she thought, "the way I see him the most."

She stood in the doorway between her office and her computer room and sipped a cup of nearly warm green tea.

"Hanging out, waiting for me to be finished with my patients."

The woman smoothed the front of her white lab coat and tasted her tea and thought how the big chocolate Lab was about seven now, middle aged and slowing down. Getting a little grizzled around the muzzle, looking very wise and worldly. Still strong and healthy and alert, but more dignified, controlled and calm.

"Is he waiting for me?" she thought to herself. "Is he dreaming? Grateful?"

The woman was by nature and by calling a healer. From her earliest memories, she had fixed her mind on medicine and being the one that helped the ones who hurt. Something in her couldn't bear suffering and pain in others. Something else inside her told her that she had the power to mend, to ease, to cure.

"Does he think about me when I'm away?" she wondered. "Does he listen for my voice and my steps? Does he know that I'm nearby?"

The woman remembered bringing home the big brown dog. How the rescue folks had warned her. Warned her that his life had been so bad. Abused, neglected and mistreated.

The corners of her mouth turned down and she absent-mindedly shook her head. She understood herself quite well and knew that this was exactly the dog for her. The one that needed her love and care and a gentle hand. The one that needed to learn to trust again. The one that needed healing.

"I wish that I could touch his mind," she thought, "the way he's touched my heart."

* * *

"She's coming," he thought as he heard her footsteps just outside the door. He exhaled gently and relaxed and settled fully onto the thick, worn mat.

"She'll come to see me and pet me and talk to me. She'll scratch the place behind my ear and she'll say my name."

He sighed again and settled in and thought about the woman. About how tired she could get, but how she always found the time for him. How he could smell the medicine and the lingering illness scent that often followed her.

"Will she be sad today? Or happy?" he wondered. "Is she tired again?"

The dog was by nature and by deed, a healer. From his puppy days he sensed the people's moods. He sensed when they were troubled, sad or hurting. He was drawn to them in a way he could not understand. He offered them his paw, his head, his heart. He believed that he could draw their pain away into himself. Something deep inside his nature told him that this was his job.

"Does she think about me when she's away?" he wondered. "Does she worry about me?"

The dog remembered all the rough times she'd been through. He remembered the demands of family and job. The great sadness that she was forced to carry with her often. And he remembered the joy that he could bring her.

His tail gave a subtle wag against the mat. He really didn't understand it all, but he knew that he could help her. In spite of all the times the others had abused him and violated his trust, he knew that for her it was different. She needed his steadiness and gentle strength. She needed him to always be there.

"I wish that I could touch her mind," he thought, "as clearly as she has touched my heart."

WALKING WILLA
by: Walt Zientek

She woke with that familiar tightness around her head. The feeling that her brain was just too full and couldn't tolerate another thought. The young dog saw that she was awake and gently nuzzled her face, licked her cheek and thumped a heavy tail against the bed frame.

The woman's hands were soon lost in the dog's warm fur and she never noticed the tightness in her head had disappeared.

As the woman prepared to leave her home, rampant, unwelcome thoughts filled her with a familiar dread. Her stomach tightened just a bit and the room turned warm. Warmer than the day.

The dog bounded into the room and quickly realized that they were going out. She jumped a bit and spun around and butt-tucked joyfully around the house. The woman laughed and called to the dog and spoke softly, telling her about the great adventures they would face that day.

As she spoke to the dog, she never noticed that her stomach had settled down and the room had once again become comfortable and cool.

As the pair approached the dog park, the woman felt her legs go heavy and weak. Instantly, the dog tugged and strained against the leash, happy to see and hear her canine friends.

The woman jogged behind the excited pup until they entered the gate. She unclipped the lead and let the dog run free amongst the other dogs. New people-friends waved and called to her and she smiled warmly and called back to them as she hurried in their direction.

She didn't notice how light and strong her legs had become. She never noticed how clear her head was, how still her pulse. She noticed the joy in her dog's body language. She noticed the gentle tones and soft support shown by her new human friends. She noticed the fresh air and blue sky and gentle breezes.

She never noticed that the terror was gone.

If you are ever to see her, give a wave and say hello. Take a moment from your life to say a word or two.

Oh, you'll know her by the way she carries her head so high, the hint of a triumphant smile across her lips. By the strong and steady pace she keeps. You will know that it is she. She'll be walking Willa.

THE ALL-NEW POLITICALLY CORRECT BREED STANDARD

by: Walt Zientek

The following Standard is merely a suggestion. Feel free to exercise your right to modify the Standard to suit your individual taste. We apologize ahead of time for offending ANYONE!

General Appearance: Can be that of a strongly built, short coupled, very active dog. It CAN, however, be leggy, weedy, sleepy, dopey or lazy looking. It MAY be wide over the loins, but remember tight abs DO indicate fitness and body awareness.

Head: Each dog SHOULD have one. If it does it will probably contain two eyes, one nose and a mouth. One ear on each side would be nice, at least for a sense of balance, but is not mandatory.

Expression: Please feel free to express yourself! It simply isn't healthy to keep things bottled up inside!

Body: Look, the media has presented an ideal that NO ONE can live up to. We have been brainwashed into self-loathing by these unreal images. We will no longer be bound to such unreachable standards! ALL bodies are BEAUTIFUL! Besides, some of us are just big-boned.

Legs and Feet: The ideal number here is four of each, but that's not written in stone or anything.

Tail: As this is a distinguishing feature of the breed we have to get a little tough on this one. (SORRY!) We must insist that the dog has one. Or had one. Or really really wishes that it did. (The committee is sorry to be so rigid, but SOME members got a little bit "testy" on this issue.)

Coats: The coat should be short, dense and free from feather BUT contemporary, ethnic and cultural styles allow for individuality. Bad-hair days are a fact of life and "bald" can be a political statement. If your Lab is so "hair challenged" that it needs to actually wear a coat, or sweater, remember that animal skins are déclassé.

Color: We simply shall NOT discriminate by color! Why, the very idea! We also formally apologize for the discrimination that has occurred in the past. We welcome Silver, Hailstone, Vanilla, Golden, Black and Tan, Blue Merle, Pied, ASCOB, Blue, Cream, Harlequin and Mauve to our ranks.

Movement: This isn't ABSOLUTELY necessary. It is simply easier if the dog doesn't have to be carried into the ring.

On the other hand, it would be nice if those dogs that are shall we say "active" could stop moving long enough for the "facilitator" to look.

(Note: the word "judge" has been changed to "facilitator" as it is far less judgmental.)

Weight and Size: (See: Body)

Faults: Offending anyone.

Disqualifications: No dog shall be disqualified for any reason. We certainly don't want to lower anyone's self-esteem.

EVERYMAN
by: Walt Zientek

"Everyman" has never been to a dog show.

"Everyman" thinks a 'Major' is a soldier on his way up.

"Everyman" thinks a CD is a good way to save money and a great way to listen to music.

"Everyman" remembers when GSDs were athletes, Setters were hunters and Boxers, Airedales and Cockers were the neighborhood nannies.

"Everyman" remembers Rin Tin Tin, Lassie, Old Yeller, Asta and Cleo.

"Everyman" remembers instinctive hunters, herders, protectors and pals.

"Everyman" is a mom in a mini van on her way to the Vet, a grandpa raking leaves with his old boy nearby.

"Everyman" is a toddler in a pet shop with her face pressed tight against the glass, a wheelchair-bound teen with his hand wrapped tight around the harness, and a young wife, home alone, feeling safer with the dog at her feet.

"Everyman" puts bows on a Yorkie, sweaters on a Frenchie and fresh food on the floor every day.

"Everyman" wants to understand why a $500.00 dog comes with more restrictions than a $30,000.00 car. Or a $200,000 house.

"Everyman" doesn't plan to breed his dog, but somehow, resents being told he can't.

"Everyman" needs an education, not a lecture, an attitude or a scolding.

"Everyman" wants a perfect pet and companion.

"Everyman" is a genius ... an innocent ... and a fool.

DOG LETTERS
by: Walt Zientek

Boy, we sure do have a bunch of letters to put before and after a dog's name. CGC and WC. CH and FCH. CDX, UD, LMNOP. I guess the dogs don't mind and it sure seems to make the owners happy, so I suppose we can go on adding more letters and inventing more things to win, more titles to earn.

You have to give the folks who earn those letters a lot of credit. After all, they did the breedings (or at least "arranged" them). They spend the money and the hours of training and practicing. They all work darned hard to get those letters attached to their dogs.

I don't.

I invented my own letters and all my dogs have earned them. You will never see those letters on a registration or a pedigree or in an ad in a dog magazine. Nevertheless, they are the letters I attach to my dogs. I don't earn them. They do.

All my dogs were and are FM, Family Members.

You see, as Family Members, they have to learn to live alongside all the other Members, two-and four-legged. They have to get along, share space, be reasonably behaved and show some manners.

The best part of this title is the fact that you too can award it to your dog. You never pay anything, send in verification or stand out in the rain, unless of course you want to.

Also the rules are sort of loose. Whatever your family decides is just fine. When your dog meets those standards, just slap those letters right on. Here are a few of the standards we use around here. Remember, these are for illustration purposes. Feel free to use or disregard.

THRESHOLD TEST: Dog NEVER goes through a door or a gate without a leash. Can't be a Family Member if you run away or get hit in traffic. We really work on this one.

COMPANY IS HERE TEST: People can actually walk into your home without being mugged. Grandmas do not get knocked over. Crotch sniffing is held to an absolute minimum. Happy tail wagging and butt shaking are acceptable, friendly greetings.

TRASH CAN TEST: Garbage stays IN the can. Period. It ceases to be "food" once it hits the receptacle.

KITCHEN TABLE TEST: People sit at kitchen table and enjoy a meal and conversation. Dogs do not. Actually very easy to train, except for humans who offer scraps to the dogs from their seats. Swatting these folks with a newspaper is an acceptable correction.

SAFE COUNTERS: If counters were made for dogs they would be much lower and easier to access. They, however, were made for people and are way up in the air. There is a simple logic to this.

WEAVE TEST: Unlike the usual tests where a dog has to weave around some poles, or heel around a couple of volunteers, in this test, the dog must weave its way around all the people-things in your home without destroying them. Shoes, belts, hairbrushes and underwear don't belong on the floor. But because in the real world people often are careless or sloppy, these things and many others find themselves in a dog's path. The dog must learn to disregard. Again, this is a simple test, easy to train. It is the people who seem to never learn.

Other tests include the "WALK AROUND THE BLOCK WITHOUT BREAKING MY ARM" test, the "RIDE IN THE CAR" test, the "SMALL CHILDREN IN THE HOME" test, the "THAT'S THE CAT'S FOOD" test and the "STOP BARKING AT THE NEIGHBORS" test.

Feel free to go ahead and use what you want. Ignore the ones that you don't care about. Add more. We always give the FURNITURE DISCRIMINATION test, the one that tells the dog which things are for people only, but that may not matter to your family. Be creative. When your dog learns the rules to being a good member of YOUR family, put the FM letters on its name.

Those are the ones that count the most.

GRAYBEARD AND THE MYSTERY LADY
A GRAYBEARD AND YELLOW DOG STORY
by: John Arrington

There is something about her. Something that attracts his attention. Graybeard pushes his cart with the wiggly front wheel through an aisle lined with brightly colored cereal boxes. Ahead of him, studying the fine print on a box of "Organic Bran" stands a hefty woman, fair-haired and plain featured. What is it about her? Graybeard passes the stranger and turns the corner at the end of the aisle.

"Organic Bran, huh?" Graybeard smiles broadly. "Maybe that's what I noticed about her," he chuckles.

He sees her again in fresh meats and then amongst the lettuce and cauliflower. He names her Mystery Lady. There is something about this plain looking woman that interests him. It isn't sexual. Graybeard is old but he still understands the difference between a turn-on and simple curiosity. As he advances through canned vegetables, his mind spins. Like a song you can't get out of your head, Graybeard can't get Mystery Lady out of his mind. What is it about this lady?

"Maybe she waits on me in a store I patronize," he wonders in the baking supplies and syrups aisle, but discards the idea before he gets to the plastic bottles filled with yellow salad oils. He is passing gallons of bottled mineral water when Mystery Lady comes around the corner at the other end of the aisle. She stops, pulls a bag of "Organic Corn Chips" from the shelf and drops it in her shopping cart. Their eyes meet for an awkward instant. They both look away and pretend the eye contact is accidental.

Graybeard pushes his orange plastic cart up to the conveyer belt and begins unloading. The check out lady is worth checking out. Graybeard grins. It isn't the express lane so he can check out as many items as he likes. He is just getting into a delicious fantasy that involves Check Out Lady and a large bottle of "Organic Canola Oil" when Mystery Lady appears in the check out lane next to his. The fantasy dissolves into a sea of unanswered questions about Mystery Lady. There is something? He just can't put his finger on it.

The groceries are paid for and bagged. The automatic doors part. Mystery Lady cuts him off with a deft maneuver at the edge of the big rubber non-skid mat. Graybeard brakes hard and stops his cart. Mystery Lady brushes past him in a hurry to get somewhere. "My, that "Organic Bran" is fast acting stuff," he chuckles.

Then he knows. He knows what it is about Mystery Lady that caught his eye. Of course! It was right there in front of him. She is wearing a navy blue fleece jacket made from one of those plush velvety looking pile fabrics. That's what it is. Mystery Lady is wearing a fleece jacket and it doesn't even have one single solitary dog hair on it anywhere. No kidding! Not a dog hair anywhere!

Graybeard looks down at his sweater. It is covered with Yellow Dog's hair. Mystery Lady is loading groceries into the back of a big green Suburban. A gentle breeze blows in her direction. Graybeard brushes his hands vigorously on the front of his sweater. A small blizzard of yellow dog fuzz drifts on the wind towards Mystery Lady. Some falls on the navy blue fleece jacket. It is no longer pristine. The jacket has come of age. Mystery Lady has been baptized.

Graybeard smiles. He has done his part. The gods are happy.

Graybeard and Yellow Dog are fictional characters loosely based on the events surrounding the life of John Arrington and his crack research assistant, a yellow Labrador Retriever named Chamois.

GOOSE BUMPS
A GRAYBEARD AND YELLOW DOG STORY
by: John Arrington

Raindrops dance on the surface of the pond. A man with a gray beard and a yellow Labrador Retriever walk a narrow path that leads into the marsh. A flotilla of mud hens paddles past a clump of cattails. In the distance, geese flap and cry to one another. Graybeard raises a pair of binoculars and finds their formation. Goose bumps trace a path down his spine. Yellow Dog raises her head to watch the flight of wild things as they pass overhead. A pair of woodpeckers flits from branch to branch. A flash of pure white on the far side of the marsh catches Graybeard's eye. The binoculars tell him it is an egret fishing for frogs.

Yellow Dog stops frequently to taste the smorgasbord of scents. Graybeard pauses to hear the music of the marsh. Small birds, frogs, ducks, geese, wind in the trees and the rain on water play nature's melody. A squall ruffles the surface of the pond. Wind driven rain stings his face. He draws the hood of his parka close and smiles. Cold wet weather insures their solitude.

Yellow Dog drops a stick on Graybeard's black rubber boot. It is an invitation to play. They stand on a narrow dike at the water's edge. "Heel," commands Graybeard. The dog sits on his left. The stick flies from his hand. Yellow Dog watches the flight and marks the fall. Does she pretend the stick is a warm, fat duck? Graybeard marvels at the primordial beauty of a Labrador Retriever bounding though chest deep water on a stormy winter day. A pair of ducks explodes from the cattails, startling the dog and the man. More goose bumps!

Yellow Dog sleeps beside his chair and dreams of fat ducks hiding in the cattails. She moans and yips. Her feet move as if she were running. Graybeard gently strokes the soft fur on the dog's head and remembers the three Labs that came before her. They are gone now, but when he walks in the wild places he feels their presence, he remembers their joy and enthusiasm.

His eyes close and he daydreams of other cold wet days, of marshes and mountain meadows, and adventures shared with Labrador Retrievers. The memories warm his soul and give him goose bumps.

Graybeard and Yellow Dog are fictional characters loosely based on the events surrounding the life of John Arrington and his crack research assistant, a yellow Labrador Retriever named Chamois.

BELLY RUBS AND PEANUT BUTTER
AND JELLY SANDWICHES
A GRAYBEARD AND YELLOW DOG STORY

by: John Arrington

Lead a blindfolded person into a garage and ask them to identify where they are. Nine out of ten will tell you they are in a garage. Garages have a distinctive if not unpleasant odor. It is a concoction of rubber tires and petroleum products, lawn food and laundry soap, dust and mildew. Graybeard's garage smelled that way. He liked the garage. It was a man's kinda place filled with manly stuff. He supposed the feminists would take issue with that. His perception of what makes a place manly had been formed long ago. It was too late to change.

A load of dog towels was in the washing machine. Graybeard's truck was backed up to the garage door. He sat on the tailgate enjoying the warmth of the sun. Yellow Dog sat beside him. They were celebrating a successful day in the field with an al fresco peanut butter and jelly sandwich. She stared into his eyes with that urgent look Labs get when food is involved. Graybeard smiled and pinched off a bite of his sandwich. Yellow Dog wagged her fat otter tail and shifted her weight from one foot to the other. Graybeard smiled and teased her with the tidbit. Yellow Dog wagged harder and nodded her head at the food. Two ropy threads of drool hung from the corners of her mouth and dripped like melting icicles.

"Eee-zee, now. Eeeee-zee," Graybeard commanded as he moved the treat towards her mouth. Yellow Dog leaned forward and took the food from his fingertips with her lips.

Graybeard wiped his hand on the leg of his pants and said, "You did good today. Someday, someone just might mistake you for a retriever." That morning Yellow Dog had responded perfectly to his first-ever attempt to handle her to a bumper with a whistle and hand signals. They ignored the fact that she'd totally blown the double and needed to be handled to the memory mark. When it came to Yellow Dog's frequent screw-ups he blamed his lack of experience as a trainer. It was better, he thought, to accentuate the positive. Yellow Dog concurred.

"We've sure gotta buncha' crap out here," Graybeard said. Yellow Dog seemed to agree and gave him a big slurpie on the cheek with the fastest tongue in the West. He smiled to himself as he surveyed the clutter. In the midst of the disarray there were five brand new fluorescent orange bumpers waiting to be used for teaching Yellow Dog blind retrieves. She was almost ready, he thought.

"Are you ready for blinds?"

Yellow Dog thumped her tail and nudged his elbow with her nose. She was more interested in her share of the sandwich than orange bumpers. Her head rested on his forearm and pressed downward. The remains of the sandwich held her undivided attention. He gave her the last bite and leaned back against the truck. Yellow Dog stretched across the tailgate and rested her head in his lap. Graybeard closed his eyes and reviewed the events of the morning training session. There had been one calamity after another culminating in the blown double. Still he felt a warm glow of pride in his dog and her accomplishments. That she would respond to his whistle and hand signals seemed to him a minor miracle.

The man and his dog dozed in the warm sunshine. One dreamed of perfectly executed triples and double blinds. The other dreamed of belly rubs and peanut butter and jelly sandwiches.

Graybeard and Yellow Dog are fictional characters loosely based on the events surrounding the life of John Arrington and his crack research assistant, a yellow Labrador Retriever named Chamois.

THEY WILL SNORE IN PERFECT HARMONY
A GRAYBEARD AND YELLOW DOG STROY
by: John Arrington

Fog blankets the fields and muffles the sound of the surf. Somewhere in the throng of the vehicles a dog yelps. In the distance, the thud of a 12-gauge shotgun sounds. The delicious aroma of freshly brewed coffee wafts from the Lions Club snack truck. Graybeard and Yellow Dog sit on the tailgate and watch the parade of vehicles and people filling the parking area. An enormous Ford Excursion SUB (sport utility behemouth) pulls into the space next to them. Its occupants emerge unwrinkled, pristine, and camouflaged from head to toe in catalog layouts. Their chocolate Lab is named Hershey, of course. Graybeard chuckles and names Hershey's humans Buffy and Jody Orvis. They approach Graybeard with questions. It is their first hunt test. Buffy and Jody are from San Jose and, "just exhausted," after their 4-hour drive. Graybeard smiles to himself and remembers the two-day drive that brought him here.

Graybeard and Yellow Dog are in pursuit of the third leg of the four required to earn an AKC Junior Hunter title. They left Boise on Thursday after work and drove over three hundred miles across the high deserts of eastern Oregon before spending the remainder of the night camped at Goose Lake on the Oregon-California border. Another long drive on Friday brought them to Eureka, California. This morning they were up before dawn and headed for the hunt test grounds on the shores of the Pacific. They are here to measure the results of their summer field training activities. Of equal importance is the opportunity provided to visit and enjoy old friends both human and canine.

Graybeard and Yellow Dog stand in a holding blind. Hershey is having trouble with the first mark, an easy 60-yard retrieve in sparse cover. His speed and enthusiasm have carried him far beyond the fall and he now hunts randomly for a bird he'll never find.

"He's out of it," Graybeard mumbles to the wind. "Too bad! Nice looking dog."

Graybeard shifts his attention to the last retrieve of the test; a one-hundred-yard-long, downhill mark over broken ground. It is the most challenging of the four singles required to pass the test and designed to answer important questions about marking ability and courage. The line to the bird is defended by clumps of bull thistles, waist high and nasty looking. Open ground on the right, upwind from the bird, will tempt the dogs to return to the area of the first mark. Dogs who risk the narrow gap between the thistles will have a better chance. With the water tests behind them, this is the mark that worries him. Yellow Dog is a great marker and he thinks she will have no trouble with the first mark, but this one looks like trouble. "Dog Twenty Nine. To the line!"

Graybeard's heart pounds. The old man and the young dog move to the line. Yellow Dog is eager, on high alert, and ready to run. She knows the men standing in the field have a duck for her to retrieve. She is eager to taste its feathers. He slips the lead from around her neck, stuffs it in his pocket and grasps Yellow Dog's red collar just in case. They are ready. He signals the judge.

Out in the field the gunners rise to their feet. A big duck flies through the air. The sound of a shotgun blast shatters the quiet of the afternoon. Moments later she prances across the line with head held high and tail wagging. A much relieved old man with a gray beard hands the duck to a judge and lines her up with the gap between the thistles.

"One more to go and they saved the hardest for last," he mutters.

A black ribbon on asphalt stretches to the horizon. There are no power lines or even fences here, just a lonely stretch of highway through the sagebrush. It is the easiest kind of driving, the kind that allows the mind to wander. Graybeard is reminiscing, remembering details from the test. Details like the long line of dusty vehicles lurching up the rutted dirt road at sunset and how the soft light of the setting sun bathed the hills and forests in shades of orange, and rose pink, and soft purples. His stomach was full of barbecured salmon then. Now it is empty and rumbles. The nearest fast food is still 150 miles away. They pass through the town of Alkali, population 2, at 85mph.

Yellow Dog is a good traveler. She wears a harness and is connected to the seat belt and sprawls across the seat resting her head in his lap. Graybeard looks down at her and remembers the look of pride in her eyes when she delivered a soaking wet duck to his hand. Water had been her nemesis since an ear infection, long since cured, and cold water convinced her that swimming caused pain. The long summer of water work and maturity had changed all that. She still enters the water with caution, a fact he laments, but when there are birds to retrieve she forgets the sting of cold water in an infected ear. Graybeard strokes her soft fur and smiles. Yellow Dog thumps her tail on the seat and licks his hand.

An hour later they pass through Wagon Tire. Graybeard hardly notices signs proclaiming the entire town for sale. Instead he relives that last difficult retrieve. Yellow Dog had run right at and then between the bull thistles and disappeared into the cover on the direct line to the bird. Moments that seemed like hours elapsed before she emerged with a duck clenched between her jaws. But it wasn't over yet. She still had to deliver it. He wouldn't relax until she was at heel and the bird was in his hand.

Yellow Dog sits up in the seat now, long ropes of drool hang from her jowls. Graybeard munches on an apple and chunks of cheddar cheese. Yellow Dog looks at him using every subtle trick in her repetoire to convince him that she will die at any moment without food. He is an easy target today and feeds her bites of apple and cheese and pets her and lets her get away with forbidden behavior. She licks his ear and drips drool on his sholder. Graybeard fends her off and looks at the speedometer, then at the rearview mirror from which a garish orange rosette ribbon dangles. A lump forms in his throat. His eyes are moist and happy. He swallows hard and dabs at his eyes with the back of his hand.

The old man and the yellow dog will sleep in their own bed tonight. He will dream of their perfect day. She will dream of fat ducks and chunks of chedder cheese. They will snore in perfect harmony.

Graybeard and Yellow Dog are fictional characters loosely based on the events surrounding the life of John Arrington and his crack research assistant, a yellow Labrador Retriever named Chamois.

TALKING DOGS
by: Walt Zientek

I suppose thousands of years ago nomadic tribes of humans, hunter-gather types, journeyed through rain forests and savannas, scaled mountains and glaciers and crossed frozen tundra and burning sands. I suppose their dogs traveled with them.

Our primal ancestors would meet up with friendly groups and settle around a blazing fire, with their dogs close by. People being people, I bet their talk often turned to dogs.

Talking about which dogs could track game and run it to the ground or to their spears. Which dogs would guard and protect their clans as they slept. Which dogs could stand the cold and snow. Which could fight. Which were best for food.

As time wore on and man became more sophisticated and somewhat more civilized, his dogs came along and became more specialized. Warriors would breed and train their great Mollosser curs and when they gathered, they would brag about their bloodlines and breed them to the strengths of others. And set them off to fight each other.

In other places, around other fires, shepherds bragged about the herding dogs, the guardian dogs. Monks and Holy Men discussed and refined the breeding of some little warning dogs with magnificent coats, to be given as the gifts of kings and royals. Other Holy Men in other worlds discussed the dogs of burial and sacrifice.

Wherever men and women have gathered, the dogs and conversation have followed. They have argued, bragged and competed; dog against dog, vermin, badger, wolf, lion, bull and bear. Even against other men.

Dogs, being dogs, have followed mankind into the computer age. The age of the Internet. The age of electronic mail and communication. Now people from all over the world form Dog Lists, discussion groups. Via e-mail, they instantly communicate with others in their extended clan to talk about their dogs. No longer do they have to risk the journey over perilous terrain. No longer do they risk topography and weather.

But still they gather, crossing oceans, mountains, deserts, and continents. Still they sit, talking dogs.

THE CAMPFIRE
by: Walt Zientek

Come on Caleb, sit here a minute. Good boy. Wait while I put some kindling down. You know, we all used to sit around this old campfire. Hard to believe, I know. Folks would see the light from this fire all round the world. It was like a beacon, calling kindred spirits to come and sit a while and sometimes talk about the things we cared about.

I know it seems hard to believe, the way things are going now, but it sure is true. Why folks used to make up songs and we all sang them. Others would ask for prayers and, no matter what way we saw God, we all prayed for them. When a tragedy struck, we sat a little closer threw more wood on the fire for warmth and put an arm around the folks who needed it.

Some folks had a lot to say, some just sat here every night and stared into the flames, feeling the warmth and learning from others. Sometimes groups would bring up a subject that others didn't care too much about, but everyone would listen and wait for something new. Sometimes groups would talk privately, but they always returned to the campfire.

Hang on fella, I need to add a little more wood. I sure hope this catches!

Yep, this old campfire was a heck of a place. We had new folks come round every night. We always made room for them, always found them a log to sit on, always listened to their stories. We were always sad when someone left. Felt like we lost a family member. But, like all families, we had our differences. Sometimes we couldn't resolve them. That was sad.

What happened? I really don't know. It seemed to happen so fast. Feelings got hurt somehow. Small groups got up from the fire and talked over there. Some folks just got up and walked away. It got harder to tend the fire. It started to go out. More folks got up and either walked away or found a group to join away from the fire.

Hey, I think it's burning now! Sit closer big guy. I see a few friends have seen the flames and are coming back to sit awhile. Plenty of room for everybody here. Plenty of stories to tell, plenty of silly songs to sing, plenty of things to learn.

Will everyone come back and sit around the campfire again? I don't know buddy. I'll toss on some more wood and wait ... and hope.

THE CAMPFIRE: A MID-WINTER'S NIGHT
by: Walt Zientek
for our friend and partner, John

The wind was cold, as it usually is this time of year. The campers pulled their heavy clothes tightly against their chilled bodies as they slowly made their way to the old familiar clearing.

The differences in this group were amazing. Grandparents and young mommas walked side by side. California and Florida tans beside the ashen, February pallor of New Englanders. Canadians and Scots chatted animatedly with Swedes, Aussies, Asians and Latinos. Some tall men helped some tiny ladies make their way. Healthy and vigorous, unwell and weak, all side-by-side.

Some wore the clothing of the successful: labels from the finest stores. Others making do with what they could afford. And still, they laughed and smiled and helped each other over the obstacles they encountered. They never saw their differences. Or, if they did, they didn't care.

Through the snow and ice, over deserts, mountains, plains and oceans, they steadily made their way.

Each one found a place around the roaring campfire as they loosened their heavy clothes. They always made room for newcomers. They passed around coffee, tea and sweet hot chocolate as they offered words of sympathy, encouragement and advice.

They showed photographs of the people and the pets that shared their lives. They quietly held the shoulders of a sobbing friend in need while others shook the hands or slapped the backs of those with wonderful news to tell.

The fire roared until even the coldest found some warmth. And then, a man stood up. He had a twinkle in his eye, a whistle around his neck and a young yellow Lab by his side. The fire reflected off his silver beard and the group grew suddenly quiet. All eyes and ears were drawn to the man as he looked around the fireside. From the deep side pocket of his heavy yellow slicker, he produced some rumpled sheets of paper.

"Place, Chamois," he said as the pretty yellow girl settled down.

"Hi Everyone," the man began. "My name is John and I have a story here I hope you'll enjoy..."

The wind was no longer cold. The differences seemed to all disappear. The fire roared and the campers listened and let his story weave its spell. And most of all, to take them all together to that special place that they had learned to share. And love.

CAMPFIRE 2: CLOSURE
by: Walt Zientek

"C'mon, Caleb, pull in a little closer. Gotta make a little more room. Did you ever see so many folks and so many dogs before? I told you, this old campfire is a beacon and it sure is lighting up the sky.

Listen! That group over there is singing a song about Labs. Listen to them! Ever see so many smiles? Nope, me neither.

Look over here. See that lady looking at the stars. I'll bet she sees the face of an old friend up there. Sure is good to see her here again.

Boy, the fire is really blazing! The old warmth is pushing the chill right out of the air. Warming up a lot of hands. Warming up a lot of hearts.

See those people. Those are Breeders, good ones. They sure do know about Labs. They are teaching all the new folks. Trying to help them learn the ropes. And those folks are trainers and trialers. Sharing all their tricks for free.

There's a lawyer. No, there are two. And she is a doctor and he is a writer and there are some nurses and that lady there, why, she's forgotten more about Labs than I'll ever learn!

What? You bet. Sure is good to see the family get together again.

My eyes, big guy? Just a little smoke, just a little smoke."

WALKING WITH BOB
by: Walt Zientek

We all read an e-mail message from a friend. The fact that we had never met was not important. The fact that she shared her story with us was.

She told us a heartbreaking tale of a great yellow Lab named Bob. How a tragic accident of fate and circumstance claimed him and tested her spirit and her soul.

The details of that story brought us together in many ways, across many miles. It touched a common chord and also opened many private memories. It became both a personal conduit and a universal truth. It's funny how that happens sometimes. How things become important in many different ways.

To some, Bob became a symbol. A symbol of the bond and the relationship between a dog and its owner. A symbol of trust, understanding, love, symbiosis, and probably a dozen other things.

To some, the story was more concrete. A story about a good dog gone, lost too young; an owner's broken heart. A lesson learned the hard way. The sad way.

Some folks found an old, painful, personal memory and reflected on an old friend. Others just imagined and empathized, and for a moment understood the fear and grief and loss.

In its way, the story of Bob brought a lot of different people together. It reminded us all of our values and showed us a bit of our own humanity and our spirit. I guess it helped to remind us of what really is important.

Like the typical Lab that he was, Bob found a way to

touch us all. Even those he never met. And for a brief instant, we all held his leash and took a collective walk with a good dog. We all took a walk with Bob.

A DOG WRITER'S 'TAIL'
by: Walt Zientek

The tall man sat at his keyboard. His wife was working and his daughters at college. He had just spent some quality time with his dogs. This meant that they were tired and resting at his feet. It also meant that he was exhilarated and filled with that old familiar feeling. A story was about to be born.

And while his dogs, those nearby and those remembered, were always the inspiration for his works, he could never write in a personal, narrative style. He had to distance himself a bit in order to keep a balance. In order to keep perspective. In order to keep emotions from swallowing his words.

He tried to squeeze meter and balance from prose until an essay felt a little like a poem. He forced the feelings onto the page and prayed it said what really couldn't be written. He hoped the readers would hear it with their hearts as they read it with their eyes.

Sometimes he succeeded. And when this happened, he soared. For he had found a tiny, universal truth that linked people of different places and lives, to a common understanding.

Sometimes he failed. And when this happened, he crashed. For his weakness with words somehow hurt or troubled or confused someone who didn't deserve this pain.

But, because he knew himself so well, he wrote on. And hoped that next time he would paint a clearer picture. And choose the perfect words. And touch, at least a little, on the relationship of man and dog.

This time, however, the rules had changed. The readers wanted game and sport. Oh, he understood. He understood the nature of competition. He understood that it often brought out the worst in himself. The obsessive desire to be the best in everything he did. The need to win.

He didn't much like that side of himself. At least not where dogs and writing were concerned. That wasn't what it was all about.

The tall man sat at his keyboard, shook his head and sighed quietly. He really didn't have a choice. Because he really did know himself so well, he closed the screen ... and walked away.

THE OPEN GATE
by: Walt Zientek

She wasn't the biggest. Or the smallest. But she sure was the sweetest. Soft black fur, so shiny, it nearly glowed. That slightly worried brow with deep, dark eyes that gave her a 'please love me' look.

She wasn't the boldest. Or the most timid. But she was the friendliest, people loving-est, trusting-est one. The one with all the promise to do or be whatever was asked.

A truly loving family took her home. And gave her love. And training. And a name. The family gently taught her the rules. They taught her which things were toys and good to chew. They showed her where her warm, safe bed was kept.

Her family got her vaccinations and special, very expensive food to eat. They taught her games like hide-and-seek, get-the-ball and going-for-a-ride.

She got to go to puppy school and training classes. She

got new collars as she grew. She loved her home, her kids, and her yard.

Then, one day, someone left the gate ajar. It wasn't on purpose, it just didn't catch.

Chasing butterflies around the yard she found herself at the open gate. She looked. She sniffed. She put her nose into the wind and sniffed again.

And then she sat. And barked. And barked and barked until her owner came and latched the gate and said the 'Good Girl' words.

Sometimes you get lucky.

Sometimes you need a happy ending.

THE HAUNTED BOWL
by: John Arrington

It's not much to look at. Just a big old cream-colored bowl. You know, one of those old fashion crock bowls with a shiny glaze except on the bottom and around the rim. It's thick and heavy with short vertical sides. For almost thirty years that old bowl has occupied a place on my kitchen floor. It came from Jackson's Hay and Feed, one of those tin-roofed feed stores, the kind with a dusty wooden floor, the pungent aromas of alfalfa and bags of feed, and the sounds of cheep-cheeping fuzzy yellow chicks in an incubator. At $4.95 it represented a major investment for a college student drawing $90.00 a month on the GI Bill.

Today, it came out of the cupboard where it was stored after Cheddar, my dear old yellow Lab, had to be put down. Somehow it just seemed too big to feed the puppy from until now. The puppy, another yellow girl I named Chamois, is growing fast. Now, at almost 18 weeks of age, she's ready for the bowl. She'll be the 3rd Lab to eat from it.

Swamp was the first. For 13 years Swamp ate her meals from the bowl. Now as I look at it sitting on my kitchen floor, I can see Swamp as clearly as if she were here. She liked to lie on the floor with the bowl between her front legs when she ate. Her last meal came from that bowl. Hill's k/d I think it was. A special food for dogs with failing kidneys. She'd been on the k/d since September. The vet told me she had about 4 months left so I started looking for a puppy.

Swamp rode with me out to a farm on a windy Kansas

prairie. The farmer had about ten kennel runs. On one side were Labs and on the other were pointers. "I breed 'em to put meat on the table," he said, "and I don't usually sell 'em to people who don't hunt." I confessed I was not a hunter, but Swamp worked her magic on him and soon we were driving home with a precocious yellow puppy we named Cheddar.

The bowl got Cheddar in trouble. She tried to eat from it when Swamp was holding it between her paws. A quick growl and a snap of Swamp's powerful jaws and we were racing to the vet's for a couple of stitches on her nose. I hadn't thought of that for years. Now with the bowl sitting here on the kitchen floor, it seemed like yesterday. And, as if it were yesterday, I again experienced the sharp pangs of grief felt so many years ago when we drove Swamp to the same clinic and said good-bye. That night Cheddar ate her first meal from the bowl and for the next 15 years it was filled for her every morning.

Cheddar's technique was different than Swamp's. She'd walk up to the bowl, get a chunk or two in her mouth and walk away as she crunched the kibble. Then she'd circle back for another bite. She always ate half of the food in the morning and the other half just before bedtime. It was a pattern that never varied.

The old five-dollar bowl is probably the only thing I still own that was mine 30 years ago. It has served us well and tonight Chamois will eat her first meal from it. I wonder if she knows how valuable it is and what it means to me? I wonder if she knows it's Halloween and that her meal tonight will be served in a haunted bowl; a big old cream-colored bowl haunted by the ghosts of Swamp and

Cheddar and a thousand poignant memories. Will she know as she eats that a black ghost will lie down and wrap her front legs around the bowl and that a yellow ghost will grab a bit and then circle back for more. Will she see the tears in my eyes before I turn away and stare into the past? Or will she just devour the food, lick her chops, and wag her busy tail?

The Haunted Bowl

WINTER NOSES
by: Walt Zientek

My yellow guy's got perfect size,
Double coat and deep dark eyes,
Otter tail, coupled short,
Built for either ring or sport,
Level topline, balanced head;
But why the hell's his nose so red?

Metal dish and lots of kelp,
Doesn't seem to be much help!
Take him outside, let him run
In the frozen winter sun,
Put a lamp right near his bed;
The silly thing is still bright red.

Nothing much that you can do,
Short of polish for your shoe,
Nothing in the food or drink,
Keeps the nose from turning pink.
Remember summer's coming back,
And the nose will turn to black!

BLACK LABS vs. YELLOW LABS
by: John Arrington

The storm raged on for 3 days and so did the argument about which was better, black Labs or yellow Labs. We were confined to the cramped quarters of a two-man mountain tent filled to capacity with two men, two Labs, and as much gear as we could squeeze inside. An unexpected August snowstorm in the High Sierra had us pinned down. We passed the time by telling lies about the dogs and arguing over which color is the best.

"You know time was when Labs were Labs and Labs were black. Period." My companion said. "Yellows might be Labs, technically, but real Labs are black. Everyone knows it. Chocolates by the way are something you give your wife for Valentines Day. Nope, in my father's day if you owned a Lab, you had a tough black dog that slept outdoors and it could retrieve dead ducks in icy water all day long. Labs were tough black huntin' dogs and not at all like those sissy dogs you see today. Why, 'black Lab' rolls off the tongue like bacon and eggs, soap and water, salt and pepper. The rising popularity of yellow Labs signals the inevitable decline and fall of the breed."

I argued that yellows are just as smart and trainable as blacks, just as tough, easier to see in the dark, that gentlemen prefer blondes, and that yellows are infinitely easier to photograph.

As the storm intensified and the days of confinement wore on, we refined the argument until we finally agreed on the definitive answer to the question of which is better, the black Lab or the yellow Lab. Our conclusion is that yellow Lab hair looks worse on your clothing and furniture than black Lab hair. And that black Lab hair looks worse on your dinner plate.

GOOSE RAPE
by: John Arrington

Outside, the thin mountain air was filled with falling snow. The nylon tent walls flapped and shuddered with each new blast of wind. Inside the crowded tent were two humans and two black Labs. The Labs were sleeping and keeping our feet warm. We were drinking hot tea laced with sugar and 151-proof rum. It had been a long and arduous day battling the storm and the altitude. The last thing I remembered before falling asleep was how warm and comfy my brand new goose down-filled sleeping bag was.

In the morning the cursing of my friend awakened me. "!@*%&#@!* dog," he said.

"Uhhh, huh," I mumbled.

"Goose rape," he said, "looks like someone committed goose rape."

I struggled to a sitting position and slowly opened my eyes. The tent was filled with snow. Where did it come from? Then it dawned on me. I looked at the dogs. Bubba's mouth was filled with soggy down. He had white feathers stuck to his black nose. He looked at me and wagged his tail. There was an explosion of feathers. He had eaten a hole in my brand new sleeping bag.

The expression on his face said it all. "With all these feathers, there's gotta be a goose in here somewhere."

THE GREAT HIGH SIERRA MACARONI AND CHEESE DINNER-EATING CHAMPIONSHIP

by: John Arrington

No kidding! There I was! Flat on my back at 11,500 feet and laughin' so hard there were blue spots in front of my eyes. I swear to Buddha! It was the funniest thing I ever saw in my whole life. Bill's face had just gone from deep red to cyanotic blue. He was stompin' his feet and snorting like a horny donkey. He held a death grip on a giant table-spoon and a pot of macaroni and cheese. Cheesy noodles were squirting outta the corners of his mouth and ...! But I'm getting ahead of my story.

It began innocently enough. There were four of us: me, Bill and my black Labrador Retrievers, Swamp and Bubba. We'd taken two leisurely days to climb Pine Creek Pass and settle into a picturesque base camp in Royce Lakes Basin. We planned to spend a week there, day hiking, fishing, taking pictures and just enjoying the serenity and the mild High Sierra summer weather.

Now you need to know that Bill was not only a prodigious eater but also a very fast eater. He could finish a salad, main course, and 2 desserts before anyone else unfolded their napkins. Bubba, my year and a half old Lab, was also a fast eater. Bubba seldom chewed his food. Like Bill, he inhaled every edible thing put in front of him. And like Bill, he loved macaroni and cheese.

One evening after dinner we pondered over who could eat a macaroni and cheese dinner the fastest, Bill or Bubba. I supported Bubba. Bill figured he could beat the dog. The topic of who was fastest came up again and again. On our last night in the mountains two macaroni and cheese dinners were taken from our emergency food cache. The Svea stoves were started and the water boiled, the noodles cooked and the bets were placed. The losing side would pay for the traditional coming-out-of-the-mountains-feast.

We drained the noodles, added the margarine, reconstituted non-fat dry milk, the powdered cheese and stirred it all together. I held a pot of macaroni and cheese in one hand and a drooling Bubba in the other. Bill held his pot of noodles under his nose with his left hand and the king sized tablespoon in his right.

"Ok, I'll put Bubba's pot on the ground and count to three. On three, I'll release him and you both start eating. Onnnne. Twwwoooo. Three!"

Bill scooped cheese noodles into his mouth. He was chewing, swallowing, and reloading simultaneously. Bubba buried his head in the aluminum pot. The sides of his stomach were sucked in and his head bobbed as his jaws worked up and down. Bubba took the early lead. Bill scooped faster, chewed faster swallowed faster. Bubba gulped and slurped, unaware it was a contest, but he ate like an industrial strength vacuum cleaner nevertheless. In less than a minute Bubba ate 3/4ths of his macaroni and cheese. Bill was scooping faster than he could chew and swallow. His cheeks began to bulge. He looked like Dizzy Gillespie going for a high note. He did not concede. His honor was at stake. He scooped faster yet. He probably had at least 2/3rds of the noodles stuffed in his mouth. That's when I started to lose control. I couldn't help it and began to howl. Laughter is contagious and Bill started to laugh too. Tears were rolling down our cheeks. Noodles were oozing out of Bill's mouth and sliding down and then falling off his chin. Bubba was licking his pot clean. Bill still had three or four scoops to go. I tried to declare Bubba the winner, but was laughing too hard. Bubba was eating the stuff that fell to the ground. Bill looked as if he were about to spray noodles. Great bursts of surplus laughter exploded through my nose. I gasped for air. Bill chewed and tried to swallow but it was no use. The noodles were packed so tightly in his mouth he couldn't swallow. Or breathe. A noodle emerged from his left nostril. He buried his head in the aluminum pot and refilled it with half chewed noodles. I fell to the ground and rolled in the dirt holding my sides. Bill sat on a rock, took a huge and long overdue breath, and finished eating the pot of noodles. Bill never wastes food.

"Bubba won," I gasped.

"No way, I woulda' kicked his butt if you hadn't made me laugh."

"No way, you still looked like Dizzy Gillespie and Bubba was finished."

"No way."

"A noodle came out of your NOSE!"

"You made me laugh. It wasn't fair."

And though the competition was held over 20 years ago, when the coals of a campfire glow and the stories of our youth are retold, we still howl and laugh and stomp our feet and argue vehemently over the winner of 'The Great High Sierra Macaroni and Cheese Dinner-Eating Championship.'

SWAMP GAS
by: John Arrington

It happened back when I was in college. We were back-packing in the High Sierra near Lake Edison. Swamp was a young black Labrador Retriever learning to carry a dog pack. The trail was rugged and steep. By the time we reached Devil's Bathtub, a beautiful oval shaped lake nestled in a hanging valley, we were beat. It had been a long, exhausting day in the thin air near timberline. Swamp had held up a lot better than we had, but she seemed as relieved as we were to be free of the burden of her pack.

After establishing ourselves in a nice campsite, we set about preparing our evening meal. The dehydrated and freeze-dried concoctions were easy enough to prepare and pretty hard to get down. The main course was something involving noodles, cheese sauce and little leathery cubes of dehydrated chicken. It was called Chicken Romanoff. Not only was the food bland and boring, the effects of the altitude had killed our appetites. Swamp was not affected. She wolfed down her ration of dog food with gusto and helped us finish off the leftovers. She even liked the dessert we'd tasted and rejected, a concoction called 'French Apple Compote'. Not long after dark we crawled into our tiny tent, zipped up our sleeping bags. Swamp was nestled between our feet and snoring before either of her human companions could fall asleep.

Later that night I remember dreaming that I was high on the side of Mt. Everest. My oxygen tank was empty, I was gasping for air. Blue spots in front of my eyes signified an imminent loss of consciousness. I awoke with a start not quite knowing where I was. Then it hit me. Swamp gas! A cloud of stench so thick and heavy, instead of rising, it settled on the floor of the tent, displacing breathable air with something so vile it could wilt artificial flowers. My eyes were tearing and burning. My lungs ached and wheezed. I managed to recover a box of wooden stick matches from my emergency kit and burned off the gas only moments before I thought I was going to pass out. Luckily the tent didn't explode. I stubbed the match out in the decomposed granite outside the door to the tent. Hugh, my companion, stirred, grumbled, rolled over and went back to sleep.

Throughout the long night I was awakened by similar episodes and saved our lives by lighting a match. Several times through the night I also heard Hugh wake up, strike a match and then go back to sleep. In the morning we were groggy, grouchy, and suffered from terrible headaches. Just outside the door to the tent were twenty-one matchsticks planted in the ground ... a silent tribute to Swamp's fragrant reaction to freeze dried food. We renamed the food. Forevermore it would be remembered as 'Chicken Blastoff' and 'French Apple Compost.' Swamp was banned from the tent for the rest of the trip.

A HUNNERT AND TWENTY-SEVEN LABS
by: John Arrington

In was autumn in the High Sierra. Golden Aspen leaves shimmered in the crisp breeze. Rosy-golden sunlight kissed soaring granite peaks. It was a glorious day. We spent the morning struggling up the steep switchbacks of Pine Creek Pass. Our tiny caravan consisted of two hikers and two black Labrador Retrievers. The Labs carried packs loaded with dog food and a rock or two to balance their load. We carried everything else we'd need for a weeklong adventure in the mountains.

Just after lunch, the unmistakable sounds of an approaching pack train interrupted the silence. We leashed the dogs and moved to higher ground above the trail. In a few moments a string of pack mules laden with cargo and about a half dozen people riding horses came into view. The dogs fidgeted. The mules eyed them warily. We looked with disbelief at the riders. They were soft city dudes attired in the colorful clothing best suited to a golf course. The only one in the procession dressed for the occasion was the packer, a grizzled old cowboy wearing Levi's, chaps, a flannel shirt, and a battered sweat stained Stetson. A neatly waxed handlebar mustache decorated his face. His eyes were red and irritated from a lifetime of eating trail dust. A yellow hand-rolled cigarette was clenched in the corner of his mouth and he had the mean and ornery look of a desperado. The pack train stopped in front of us. The packer touched the brim of his hat and uttered a cheery, "Howdy."

Much relieved, we returned the friendly greeting and

exchanged small talk about the weather, where we were headed, the steep terrain, and the distance remaining to Honeymoon Lake where we planned to spend the night. The dudes, a captive audience clinging to the saddle horns, were silent and impatient.

The packer asked us about the dogs. How did we teach them to carry a pack? Did we have any trouble getting them "saddled up?" Where did we get their "rigs?" Did we have trouble with their feet? And finally he asked, "How much weight do they carry?"

"About fifteen to twenty pounds for the female and almost twenty-five for the male when they are in good condition," we responded.

He looked at us for a moment or two and then removed his hat and used a red bandanna to mop sweat from his bald head. He shifted his weight in the saddle and looked back at the dudes, then gently spurred his horse. The pack train started moving.

"Ya know," he drawled as they passed by, "if I got me a hunnert and twenty seven of them dogs, I could get rid of these God Damned mules".

CHAMOIS MEETS THE CHEESE MONSTER
by: John Arrington

It was Monday night and time for our first session in the Advanced Basic obedience class. The high-energy instructor lady bounced into the room and spied us. "Oh, I don't know you," she said. We were in trouble! My calm, well-behaved young dog turned into the 'Wiggle Monster From Hell' at the sound of the Teacher Lady's high-pitched voice. I glanced around the room and all the other dogs were sitting calmly beside their owners. Chamois was going ballistic! I was the only man in the room. It was going to be a long evening.

We muddled through a couple of warm up exercises and then it was time for the "stand for exam" trick. Chamois watched the other dogs and was clearly not impressed with their ability to give a stranger a warm welcome. Teacher Lady approached and Chamois gave her the full blown 'Labrador-Retriever-Welcome Wagon-Blitzkrieg' of wiggles, bumps, grinds, lunges, and a shameless display of full body wagging while nearly jerking my arm out of the socket. "Well, we have a lot of work to do, don't we," Teacher Lady said in a cold tone of voice that accused me of never ever ever teaching my dog to do anything at all. Then came a rapid-fire litany of things I must do to get my dog under control. I tried to comprehend what she was saying but Chamois was still trying to mug her. Little did I know then that Teacher Lady reeked of cheese.

Why is it, I wondered, do these women think the only way to communicate with a dog is to use a baby talk falsetto voice with a pitch somewhere between that of a mezzo-soprano and fingernails on a blackboard? Can't you just see me sitting in a duck blind with a couple of burly dudes wearing "camo" from head to toe? Chamois returns to the blind with a Mallard in her mouth. "What a goood dog-gie," I squeak in my best falsetto. The burly dudes crowd into the far corner of the blind and refuse to share their coffee.

The lesson progressed and we were doing just fine in a normal tone of voice. That is until the cheese barge approached. Teacher Lady came over to see how we were doing and again all hell broke loose. Did I tell you she reeked of cheese? I was wrong. She REEKED of cheese! And the cheese was in a bait bag hidden beneath her coat. Such a pathetic attempt at concealment won't fool Chamois and her nose was up and under Teacher Lady's coat in a flash. Of course I got another stern lecture on control and its importance. All I really needed to do was get the heck away from the cheese monster.

And so it went.

When Teacher Lady was at the other end of the line, Chamois performed flawlessly. As soon as Teacher Lady, reeking of cheese, dropped by to see how we were doing it all fell apart and I got another "helpful" lecture. The only highlight for us was a recall exercise. One by one the ladies put their dogs in a down stay, walked to the other side of the room and, using screechy falsettos, called their dog and greeted him with still more screeching. When it was our turn, Cheezilla was about as far away from us as she could be. I gave Chamois a hand signal for sit, then another for stay and walked toward the other side of the room. How long would it take her to break and attempt to mug Teacher Lady's bag of cheese? When I turned, Chamois was right where I left her. Whew! Another hand signal was all it took. Chamois sprinted across the room and skidded to a halt in front of me and sat perfectly straight.

Aww what the heck, I thought, let's show off. So I gave her yet another hand signal and she did a very nice wrap around finish. We'd just kicked butt and everyone knew it. "Now praise her," instructed Teacher Lady. She implied that I was supposed to get all wiggly and employ my falsetto. I declined the implied invitation and instead looked down at Chamois and in a normal tone of voice quietly said, "Good girl." It was enough for Chamois and she positively beamed at me and wagged her tail.

Next up was heeling "with distractions." The floor was littered with battery-operated toys that vibrated and bounced and made noises and moved around. We were to walk a weave pattern through the maze of moving noisy toys. The Springer Spaniel, so steady on the stand for exam, freaked and clung to his mom. The other dogs handled the problem with varying degrees of caution and confidence. Finally it was our turn. The Creature From The Cheese Lagoon was stationed close to the obstacle course. We approached and Chamois paid little or no attention to the toys. Instead she pulled me towards the cheese every time we passed by. I endured another lecture about control and silently wondered how Chamois would do on a duck hunt in Wisconsin? Would she retrieve a duck, or head for the nearest dairy? Such an important question begs an answer. "Control is what you want, control is what you'll get," I muttered to myself. With a devious grin on my face I started Chamois on yet another lap through the maze of noisy toys. When we got to the toy elephant, I led Chamois straight to it and said, "Fetch." Chamois' training on the walking fetch drill paid off big time. She scooped up the noisy vibrating elephant with her mouth and continued walking beside me with her shoulder perfectly aligned with my left leg. I stopped. Chamois sat. I grasped the elephant and said, "Give." She opened her mouth and turned her head away from the elephant. I put it down on the floor and we walked back to our place in line.

SOMETIMES DREAMS COME TRUE
by: John Arrington

Ok, so there we were! Standing in line waiting. Soon it would be our turn to demonstrate my yellow Lab, Chamois', proficiency in responding to my recall signal. It was the last night of our advanced basic obedience class. The teacher lady, whom I call 'Cheezilla', 'Cheese Barge', 'The Creature from Cheese Lagoon' and other complimentary names, was really outdoing herself. High pitched squeals of delight approaching sexual ecstasy were the reward for a handler or dog that did something to her liking. And all the women in class were tuned in and turned on. The dissonant chorus of ear splitting shrieks and jerky calisthenics brought to mind junior high school cheerleaders on amphetamines. A video of the commotion would be more fun than being the guest of honor at a biker's birthday orgy.

This particular recall drill required that we put our dog in a sit/stay and walk about 10 yards and call the dog. No big deal right? Wrong! Really really wrong! You see The Cheese Barge was standing half way between the dog and the handler. As soon as the dog was called, 'Cheezilla' threw four or five hunks of cheddar and a couple slices of hot dog on the floor in front of the dog. She said, "The well-trained dog will ignore all distractions and...". I never did hear the last part because of the ringing in my ears caused by 'Soprano Overload Syndrome' (SOS). No really! I heard that Teacher Lady has been served with a restraining order requiring her to refrain from speaking within 100 yards of crystal glassware. No! REALLY!

Where were we? Oh yeah. We're standing in line. My ears are bleeding. The wiggle monster from hell possesses Chamois. A serious looking lady is standing next to me. She stares into the eyes of her dog. The dog stares intently at the slimy hunk of cheese the lady holds between her lips. The lady wiggles her mouth from side to side and sucks the cheese in and out. The dog is mesmerized. I cannot begin to tell you what I was. The lady gives some kind of release signal. The dog rears up and gently takes the cheese from her mouth. Cheese-sucker Lady praises the dog with her best goochy-goo cheerleader rah-rah voice, "Guuuoood, Staaaaaaaay Feeeeeeee-FEE Pooooh." Fee-Fee Pooh ignores her and sniffs the floor in search of something else to eat. They are the star pupils.

Excuse me while I vomit.

Sorry about that. Back to the story. Soooo, one by one every dog stopped at the cheese-o-rama buffet and siphoned up a few high cholesterol snacks before returning to their owners. Cheezilla would shriek something about "more enthusiasm" and that we had to be more desirable than Limburger or Brie or something like that. Like I said, my ears were bleeding. So sure enough on the next try the sound level went up another 50 decibels. Of course the dogs still stop at the cheese and clog up a few more arteries. My mind begins to drift and I wonder if those pudgy looking show Labs that stand so still in the ring are well trained or just too full of cheese to move.

At last it's our turn. Chamois reluctantly consents to a cheap imitation sit/stay. I walk the required distance, turn, and say, "Chamois, come," in my normal tone of voice. It's like The Gunfight at the OK Corral. Cheezilla goes for her goodies. Chamois charges across the floor and skids to a halt with her nose shoved up against the bait bag. Cheezilla's hand is only half way out of the bag. She never had a chance! I can't begin to tell you how pleased I was. That I maintained a straight face without wetting myself is a minor miracle.

Of course we got the lecture about enthusiasm and being more desirable than cheese and about a bunch of other things and stuff. And we tried it again. And again. And then once more. Chamois never did make it to me without a detour through Dairy Land.

"John, you've got to show more enthusiasm," Cheezilla admonished.

"Bull@#$%," I muttered to myself in a squeaky falsetto.

Later, at home, Chamois is curled up beside my recliner. "We shall work on recalls until you can pass up a cheese and bacon sundae with peanut butter topping," I say to her. Chamois snores back at me. I close my eyes and begin to have a nightmare featuring a gigantic dragon that squirts that aerosol spray cheese stuff out of its nostrils instead of fire. Cheezilla is riding on the monster's back. She flogs its scaly sides with a cat o'nine tails wholly fabricated from Slim Jims. The dragon rears its ugly head, paws at the air, and blows two 50-pound, laser guided, cheese boogers at me. I am fatally wounded and buried in a bright yellow casket with "VELVEETA" painted on its top and sides. Cheezilla, wearing nothing more than a Green Bay Packers jersey and a cheese head hat weeps tears of whey as she reads the eulogy. "If only he'd shown more enthusiasm," she sobs, "if only he'd been more desirable than a rancid chunk of cheap cheddar, he might still be with us." Just then Chamois sticks her head under Cheezilla's jersey and gooses her with a cold wet nose to the behind. Cheezilla shrieks, loses her balance and falls into the open grave. Her neck is broken. As it happens in dreams, I am resurrected.

And sometimes dreams come true.

AN ORDINARY DAY

by: Walt Zientek

(Dedicated to Barb and Family)

"I got to spend a few minutes with a friend and colleague today. She is usually 'upstairs', teaching German and Honors English to the beautiful and gifted children of intelligent and concerned parents. I'm 'downstairs', teaching everything to (in these days of political correctness) the Special Needs kids. Hers go on to run the world, mine to the periphery of your awareness. (But that is another story, best left for another day.)

A special project gave us, and our students, some time together. She spoke to me of her old chocolate guy. At 13, he isn't doing very well. Deafness, cataracts, weakness and incontinence. Daughters who don't remember a time without the dog. A family defined, at least in part, by the relationship with a dog. It was a story long on memories but painfully short on futures.

After a while, I was aware that several students from both groups were watching us and wondering why this sweet and confident woman and this big tough guy were wiping errant teardrops from their faces.

I heard a boy, much tougher and street-wise than you or I will ever be say softly, "That's OK, mister's only talking dogs."

Are there lessons here about people and dogs and differences and a common understanding? I'm sure there are, but I'm not bright or articulate enough to sort them out. Is there poetry here? Probably not. Unless you are the kind of folks who can feel the rhythm and hear the meter in the events of a very ordinary day.

AT THE REQUEST OF FRIENDS
by: Walt Zientek

The man laughed out load. The dogs looked up, wondering what could possibly be so funny at 4:30 in the morning. A request from far away friends for poetry and stories.

The man glanced down at the four unfinished pieces on his desk and smiled and shook his head. He could barely find his coffee cup. He wondered how he'd ever find the meter or the rhyme. Or the inspiration.

The man opened his image files and brought up a photo of his dog. A simple head study of a young yellow Lab at Christmas. A toy duck between his paws, a far away look in his eyes.

"Labrador Eyes"

The man wrote on the page.

"The ancient birds of distant skies
Cross the Labrador's dark eyes."

The man wondered how and why dogs that had never hunted or even heard a gun, would stop their play and watch a formation of ducks or geese fly overhead. Why they would get a special look of recognition in their eyes.

The man re-read the words, shook his head and crossed them off. Then he wrote:

"Amidst the chaos and the strife
His eyes found all the good in life."

The man considered that perhaps that expression was something else. Maybe the calm and gentle soul that lives within the dog shows itself in the soft, warm eyes. Even, perhaps, in the silly often frantic pup, the sweet soft soul peeks out and promises the dog that lives within.

The man shook his head again and scratched away his words. He studied the photo a little more, trying to let the picture write the words, find the meter, show the theme.

"The dog sat. Quietly. Lost in a world of people things. And human dreams."

The man had tried. He closed down the picture on his screen.

He'd have to apologize to his distant friends.

There would be no story this day.

The poetry just wasn't there.

— The Request of Friends —

THEY HEAR YOU
by: Walt Zientek

The irony wasn't lost on him. Joan Baez singing "Forever Young" on the CD player upstairs, while he read mail from friends that spoke about their older dogs. Spoke about the way they didn't seem to hear as well, or at all.

His mind went back a few years, to the day it seemed his old boy stopped hearing the world. He had worked on that boy's ears twice a day, sure the infections were to blame. Perhaps they were. Or perhaps time was just beginning to claim its due.

That boy could hear a car coming minutes before it hit the driveway. He could hear a squirrel sneeze at the bird feeder, a duck quack across town, a kid sneaking down the stairs at night. Heck he could hear your words almost before you spoke them.

But that time had passed. The world became a quiet place for the old boy. His much-deserved sleep was no longer interrupted by everyday sounds. The doorbell never called him into action anymore. The shutting off of the television never called him up to bed.

The man remembered how the old dog used his eyes to keep in touch. How he watched the man move, watched his hands for signs and signals. The man remembered signaling a "sit" across the yard and the old guy dropped down, right on cue. The man remembered also that the dog couldn't hear the "Good Boy" words, so he walked across the yard, knelt down and hugged the old dog. Just to make sure the old boy knew that he was still a "Good Boy".

The man wanted to tell his friends that their dogs would

be just fine. That they would adapt to the quiet, find new ways to learn. He wanted to tell them to go ahead and use a flashlight or a laser pointer; to stamp their feet, wave their arms or try any other tricks they could.

Most of all, he wanted to tell them, that this was nature's gentle hint. That this was the time to give their old dogs a little more of their time. A little more care. A little more love. This was the time to say all the things they wanted to.

He wanted to tell them to go ahead... they still hear you.

OUR WALKS ARE GETTING SHORTER
by: Walt Zientek

Our walks are getting shorter now and taking a little longer. What used to be a race around the block is now a gentle stroll. A chance to read the messages of unseen friends who've come before. A chance to work the stiffness out. A chance to share some quiet, twilight time together.

Your naps are getting longer now. Your favorite toys no longer call you from their place. The traffic on the street outside no longer needs your watching. I wonder if your dreams are filled with memories of fields and ponds and endless runs in pain free days?

Your eyes are getting bluer now. Like autumn clouds against a cold slate sky. I know that now you see me with your nose and hear me with your heart. I wonder if you understand the things your ears can't hear me say?

Our walks are getting shorter now and taking so much longer. But I will surely slow my steps and change my pace to stay with you ... forever.

UNTIL THE DAY
by: Walt Zientek

for Sarita, Ray and Shasta

The old girl felt her worn and tired muscles relax and her pain dissolve. She drew in a long, soft breath and relaxed a little more as the familiar, loving scent of her people filled her lungs. Memories of them rushed through her brain and warmed her heart.

"A collage of happy images and tender days."

She felt their soft touches against her fur. Their hands sent a tactile message of their gratitude and their love. She felt the warmth atop her head and neck and blinked and saw their faces streaked with tears.

"Don't cry for me or feel sad."

She heard them as she shut her eyes. They said her name and the "good girl" words, through their pain and sorrow. In her mind, her tail wagged to tell them that she heard. And understood.

"Good bye, my Hearts."

She is standing in a meadow, near a stream. The sky is fiercely blue. She hears the song of many birds and smells the growing grass. Her legs are strong. Her eyes are clear. She begins to walk toward a brightly colored bridge, far off on the horizon, but pauses for a moment and looks back.

"Thank you. Until the day we walk together once again."

She turns and wags her thick strong tail and runs. And runs.

ABOUT THE AUTHORS & ILLUSTRATOR

John Arrington has been owned by Labs since he got his first Lab, a black female named Swamp in 1969. John's Labs have been his companions, backpacking and camping partners, and best buddies. "Having a Lab at my side has become one of the few constant things in my life," he says. "Relationships come and go, but you can always count on a Lab to cheer you up when you're down or to keep you company when you're lonely. I just can't imagine living without a Lab to love."

Walt Zientek is a Special Education teacher in an urban high school. He resides in Connecticut with his wife, Wendy, his daughters Cory and Jaime, his yellow Lab Caleb and a French Bulldog named Gibson. Walt is a proud winner of the Maxwell Medallion Award by the 1999 Dog Writers Association of America for his contributions to the first edition of Labrador Tales. He is also a co-author of Heart Dog Diaries, Volume 1, a collection of stories inspired by the themes in Labrador Tales. Heart Dog Diaries, Volume 1 is dedicated to raising funds for rescues, shelters and animal relief causes. His works have appeared in Labrador publications on three continents. His goal has always been to find the emotion hidden in the ordinary.

Terry Albert is an award winning writer and artist specializing in pet portraits. After a 20-year career in retail advertising, she has turned to her first love, animals. Albert provided illustrations for the 1994 Labrador

Retriever National Specialty poster, and sweatshirt and tee-shirt designs for the 1999 and 2000 National Specialties. She is a member of the Dog Writer's Association of America, and Colored Pencil Society of America. Ms. Albert is also active in Labrador Retriever and Collie rescue, and competes in obedience and field events with her dogs. She shares her home with her husband Dennis (a very understanding supporter!), two horses, three cats, four dogs, and two rescued box turtles!